Shakespeare On Celluloid

Edited by
Neil E Béchervaise

With feature chapters by
Neil Béchervaise, Joe Belanger, Bill Davison,
Dennis Robinson and Ken Watson.

St Clair Press Pty Ltd
1999

© 1999 Neil Béchervaise, Joe Belanger, Bill Davison, Dennis Robinson and Ken Watson

ISBN 0 949898 90 2

St Clair Press Pty Ltd
ACN 003 829 043
PO Box 287, Rozelle 2039 NSW Australia
Phone: (02) 9818 1942 ❖ Fax: (02) 9418 1923
e-mail: stclair@australis.net.au ❖ www.stclairpress.com.au

Cover Design:
Propaganda/goose, PO Box 161, Glebe 2037 ❖ Ph: (02) 9660 0037 ❖ Fax: (02) 9552 1714
Cover Photography:
Richard III: Laurence Olivier as Richard III (London Films Productions, 1955)
Photographs Page
From Neil Armfield's production of *Twelfth Night* (photographs courtesy of Producer, Don Catchlove)
Laurence Olivier as Richard III and Ralph Richardson as Gloucester (London Films Productions, 1955)
Printing:
Aviweb Printers Pty Ltd, 181 Glebe Point Road, Glebe 2037 ❖ Ph: (02) 9692 8531 ❖ Fax: (02) 9692 9610
Rapid Reprographics P/L, 8-10 Berry St, North Sydney 2060 ❖ Ph: (02) 9957 2345 ❖ Fax: (02) 9957 3456
Typesetting:
Propaganda/goose, PO Box 161, Glebe NSW 2037 ❖ Ph: 9660 0037 ❖ Fax: 9552 1714

Contents

Foreword

This book uses and expands reader response theory as a theoretical base. Essentially, this means that we believe that film viewers/readers bring a unique set of experiences and understandings to their reading of a film and construct the 'text' by applying these understandings to the reading. To the extent that the readers' experience and knowledge are individual, each of their readings is unique. But that is too haphazard for us as teachers. We want students to feel confident in coming to grips with the text as informed and critically resistant readers who 'know the rules of the game' of reading film as well as we expect them to know the 'rules' for reading literature. Otherwise, what is the point of being an educator?

As writers, we bring our own research of the films and a range of experience which is far more extensive than that of the average reader of a film-as-text. We also bring the language, the grammar and the ability to contextualise which we model for students and beginning film readers. Without this modelling, they have no agreed framework upon which to build and against which to confirm their own developing facility as film readers

Shakespeare was a commercial playwright and a theatre owner. He was in business to get crowds through the doors. He developed a new tragedy and a new comedy each season. If things worked, he ran with them. He was commercial first. As such, we believe, he would have been a film producer/director in the 1990s – perhaps in the style of Kenneth Branagh with his ensemble approach to film-making (eg, *Peter and Friends*), perhaps in the manner of Speilberg with his wide range of interests and universal issues. Film is the late 20th century medium. How should we/can we read it? This, for us, is what the book is about.

In this book we are exploring the range of translations of Shakespearean play-texts which have been made on film. We have focused on the readily available films and refer in passing to others we know but which may not be readily accessible.

To some extent, the approaches to the films are individualistic. We have endeavoured to meld them into a stylistically coherent structure where each chapter is written as a discussion with activities, observations and asides which extend and help to fill, for some students, what may otherwise remain as silences.

Neil E. Béchervaise
January, 1999, Vancouver

The Structure of the Book

This book is divided into five sections.

Section 1 examines the relationship between audience and performance, leading to an exploration of the differences between reading literature, play-texts and films.

Sections 2-5 identify the elements most commonly underpinning effective story-telling for entertainment: narration, spatial relationships, sequentiality and closure.

It is presumed that our readers will find many examples of every story-telling element in each of the films. In consequence, there is neither need nor intention to follow the order of presentation of the book or to use only those films discussed in each section to substantiate the focus of that section. Keen film readers will wish to add films not mentioned, or to replace films mentioned with others which seem more appropriate or appealing. We encourage this approach and wish we had more space to add extra films that we have reluctantly omitted.

The headnotes for each section have been written to stand alone. Readers wishing to apply their film reading principles to films other than Shakespearean translations will find them a useful organising guide in the development of critical film readership.

Each chapter is organised into:

Establishing Shots – focusing activities or information directed towards the fundamental concepts involved in the chapter.

Key Shots – essential definitional information.

Cutaways – student activities – leading from lower order individually focused information retrieval dependent on the student's prior knowledge and establishing a shared knowledge base, that is, establishing an entry knowledge profile for each individual student.

Director's Cuts – higher order activities promoting sharing of knowledge and processes to ensure comprehension and to promote categorisation, analysis, synthesis and informed surmise.

Section 1
Audience and Performance

Chapter 1: Reading Film as Text

Establishing Shot 1

The authors of this book have agreed that film viewing is a form of reading. To read effectively, we need to know the vocabulary, the grammar and the conventions used in constructing the text we are reading. We also need to understand the audience for whom the text is intended. Finally, we need to recognise the context in which the text is supposed to be read.

Film as a text differs from the literary text because it is written in movement, colour and sound. It is designed to be read at a single sitting at a set pace. The pace of the reading is supposed to allow all readers to feel comfortable that they are reading at their own pace. As film readers, we usually only become conscious of the complexity of what we are watching when the film has been poorly written.

This text is designed to explore the ways in which films are constructed and the problems faced by film-makers who translate plays into film. Some of the questions film-makers have to answer include:

❖ How can the intention of the play-text be translated to film?

❖ Who will be the audience?

❖ How will the play-text need to be changed to suit the grammar and vocabulary of film?

❖ How will the play-text need to be changed to suit the historical and social context in which the play will be read?

As a means of understanding the relation between the work of the playwright and of the film-maker, this text has also been designed to explore some of the central problems faced by playwrights:

❖ Who will be performing the play?

❖ Who will be in the audience?

❖ How will the play be performed?

In addressing these questions, it starts to become clear that the film-maker's concerns are remarkably similar to those of the playwright.

Translating Plays Into Film

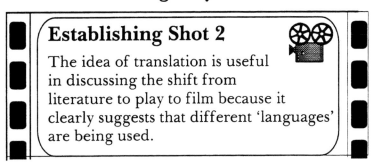

Establishing Shot 2

The idea of translation is useful in discussing the shift from literature to play to film because it clearly suggests that different 'languages' are being used.

The 'language' of literature as we recognise it is the printed text. We are familiar with the complexities of grammar and vocabulary which characterise the effective use of this 'language'. For most of us, as a result, reading the text means reading the words printed onto a succession of pages – each of which must be read before it is turned to reveal the next. Our literature reading allows us to read single words, phrases and sections. We may pause, return and even skip to establish a meaningful reading.

The play-text, however, is another language. It is intended to be seen (or heard) as the action of live players (actors) who will present an aural and/or visual text for us to 'read'. The players will not pause, stop, repeat or skip sections of the play for us to reflect or clarify our understanding of their text. Instead, working with an expanded vocabulary and grammar, or 'language' of the play, they may add tonal variation, activity, colour, light, music and sound effects to support and extend the meaning of their spoken text. Each of these elements assists us to read the play in a single performance, but the fact remains that what we cannot read in the performance cannot be repeated. We have no opportunity to return to line 53 or re-view Act 2, scene 2 to be sure that we understood what was being set up as a motivation for later action by the protagonist.

Film represents yet another language. Recorded for later transmission to an audience in the darkness and intimacy of a cinema on a large screen, the film is several steps removed from the literary text. The characters, the angles from which they are seen, their emotional relation to each other, the physical circumstances of their performance, each represents an alternative vocabulary and grammar which are selected and collected to present a single and singular reading of the text they present.

Key Shot

The film text is easily recognised as a post-modern construction: a complex series and sequence of intentions translated to celluloid as if in a single reading.

The apparent structures we translate from the screen cannot be the actual structures. We will not see the cameras, the lights, the director, the extras. We are not (at least we are not meant to be) conscious of the roles of the musicians, the editors, the colour matchers, the title designers and the hundreds of others who support the 'writing' of the film we read as a single text. The singularity of our reading of a film depends on the totality of its *constructedness*.

In the light of the cinema lobby, we recognise that we are about to see, or have just seen a complex visual and aural construction. Inside the cinema, with the lights down and our attention focused on the universe defined by the screen, we adopt a different set of semantic rules. We accept the 'reality' of the screen universe and the context in which we are being entertained. We read the film as a specialised text.

The film-maker's intention is to devise a text for which there can only be one reading. The signs we recognise in literature or in a play performance may not signify the meanings we usually provide them with. Our literary training may be consciously turned against us to create new and more complex readings. Music may suggest impending disaster. Colour may create a sense of the romantic. Camera angles may confuse our reading of power relationships.

Cutaway 1
Take 1

Remember when you were in another room and you could hear a movie on television. How did you tell what was happening or about to happen?

Was it possible to create a reasonably accurate image of what the scenery and even the actors' costumes looked like without seeing the screen?

The basic intention of the commercial film-maker is to create an entertainment which will totally engage the interests and emotions of the audience. The elements of the film are woven together to create a seamless production in which music, dialogue and images appear to have been created together. To develop a discriminating response as film readers, it becomes essential to understand the elements involved in the construction of the text. If we are to appreciate how the film is achieving its purpose, we must teach ourselves to *read against the intention* of the film-maker. In doing so, we learn to create a critical framework from within which we translate the text into a meaningful and conscious reading.

Translating Shakespeare's plays

Translating Shakespeare's plays into film presents particular problems:

❖ many people have strong feelings about Shakespeare because they once studied his plays at school;

❖ many ideas about how Shakespeare should be presented make it difficult to translate a Shakespearean play to film so that it satisfies both critics and more forgiving audiences;

❖ some people believe that because Shakespeare wrote in Elizabethan times, his plays must be presented historically.

The film translator of Shakespeare has to be both brave and talented to meet all the demands which will be made of the film.

Establishing Shot 3

Whether people speak or write or show pictures, they make choices about what to put in their message and what to leave out. The way they decide their choice seems to be very simple. But every choice makes some things important and leaves other things out. Each choice includes some readers or viewers and excludes others.

The Intended Audience

When a text is written to be read as a piece of literature, the characters, settings and events which fill the reader's mind must appear to present a reality according to the rules of reading for the reader. Some reading rules are related to the structure of written speech rather than spoken speech. Others are related to the way readers create a reality in their minds as they read.

Play-texts, however, are not usually written to be read as literature. They are more often written to be performed by actors on a stage. Readers expect to move from their home to an agreed performance area to watch the performance as audience members. *Audience expectations* may differ between individuals but the shared experience demands an interaction between players and audience. With words and action, staging, sets, lighting, costume and make-up, the actors will create a performance for readers to share in. Readers will be expected to make adjustments between the reality of what they are seeing and the reality the actors are performing.

Film demands a more distanced reading. The film audience may move to a performance space but the actors, the settings and the film-makers will not be there. Film must be read *as if* the performance space is shared between actors and audience. The reality of the film reader involves stepping through the screen into a world which has been created at another time and place.

Director's Cut 1

In Woody Allen's film *The Purple Rose of Cairo*, the hero of the film gets bored with playing the same role in every screening of the film and steps out of the screen while the film is being projected. Immediately, the film narrative is stopped as the characters on the screen, confused and then angry, try to decide what they can do without a hero. The audience for the film is equally confused and then angry.

Discuss the restrictions we place on ourselves when we read a film and then decide whether the concept explored in Woody Allen's film is a way to consider our own role as audience.

Films are made according to *rules of communication* which are as strict as the spelling and grammar rules we use to write a story, an essay or even a diary entry.

Establishing Shot 4

The choice to read a novel, a play-text or a film involves accepting a reality which is shared between the text and the reader but which only exists in the reader's mind.

Cutaway 1
Take 2

Working in small groups, list some of the different things you have to believe when you watch a film, television series or serial. Use this list to decide whether the news on television is more believable than a film which used realistic characters in real settings.

When we go to see a film in a cinema, we expect comfortable seats and the lights to be turned out; we expect the film to be in focus and we expect to be able to hear the sound track. More importantly, we expect the film to make sense to us. If things happen which confuse us or which seem unreal within the story, we may argue that the film is of poor quality. If the style of the film does not follow the usual rules for film editing and composition then, again, we may argue that the film is of poor quality. We generally *expect* to see a film which follows rules that we are already familiar with.

We *expect* characters to disappear from the screen so that we can see and hear other characters at different times and places or from different angles. We *expect* to hear music which heightens our understanding of the action and we *expect* to see colour or light and shade which match our previous understanding of how film is supposed to be. In fact, we already have a well developed understanding of the language of film.

Cutaway 1
Take 3

Have you ever watched the list of credits which come at the end of a film? Who are all of the people who are involved in making a film? List some of the tasks which are credited in every film and group them according to whether they are most directly connected with the actors, the filming, the planning, the support of the film crew and actors or the financing of the film.

Chapter 2: Macbeth

Establishing Shot

The fog clears briefly to reveal three black-clad crones dragging a sled. They stop, scratch a hole in the sand and bury a noose, a human hand and a dagger. Covering this gruesome collection, they pour blood over it, spit and speak, "Fair is foul and foul is fair/Hover through the fog and filthy air". They depart across wet, rippled sand of the beach and disappear into the fog.

Polanski's opening to *Macbeth* provides symbolic and actual references to each of the key elements of the play. More importantly, it establishes the timelessness of the action. The tide may come in to reveal the contents of the hole immediately; it may cover them more deeply. They may be revealed in some later storm. But they are there beneath the sands of time. We know they are there and we must expect them to be revealed – sooner or later.

Macbeth has been translated to film on a number of occasions but only two are readily available. Orson Welles directed and starred in the title role of his 1948 translation. Roman Polanski directed Jon Finch and Francesca Annis in a 1972 translation which was financed by Hugh Heffner (of *Playboy* fame) from a screenplay developed by Polanski and the English critic, Kenneth Tynan. The 'American gangster' film, *Joe Macbeth*, provides some interesting interpretations of events in a less text-bound or historically bound setting.

Welles' *Macbeth* is essentially a vehicle for its star while the Polanski translation is unrelentingly violent, from the first scene with the witches through the bloody battle that opens the story to the final sequence in which Macbeth is beheaded and his head carried through the streets on a pike. This chapter will concentrate on the Polanski translation which is the better known and more easily obtainable on videotape.

Key Shot

Shortly after the Polish director Roman Polanski married young film star Sharon Tate, she was brutally murdered in a ritual occult-style killing by a group of followers of Charles Manson – who is still in jail for the crime.

Macbeth is the first film directed by Polanski after this bloody ritual murder of his wife. The resulting film is particularly interesting for Polanski's treatment of the witches and for his use of violence.

Ambition and a Touch of Witchcraft

A Shakespearean tragedy is created when one or several people in important roles have too much of an otherwise admirable characteristic. Romeo and Juliet loved wisely but not well. *Macbeth* is usually accepted as a tragedy of over-ambition. Like most of the Lords of the time, probably, Macbeth would have been quite an acceptable king. He has an excellent reputation as a general; at the beginning of the play he has just saved King Duncan from certain defeat when the Thane of Cawdor turned traitor and sided with the King's enemies. He has been rewarded with that Thane's title. It seems reasonable that he might, some day, become king. As a result, when he writes a letter to his wife, she accepts his dream of becoming king. However, she also recognises that he is not politically ambitious enough to push himself towards the role. Instead, she develops a plan of her own: to kill the present King and install her husband in his place.

In Elizabethan times, to kill an annointed king was an appalling act, and Macbeth clearly recognises this fact. Lady Macbeth, however, is more ambitious than her husband. She sweeps aside his arguments and demands that he 'look like the innocent flower but be the serpent under it'. Her role in the murder of King Duncan is central to the achievement of Macbeth's ambition, but she does not have to work alone.

The witches in Polanski's *Macbeth* are ugly and eccentric but they do not perform any particular magic. When Macbeth meets them and later follows them into their cave, he is fed a soup, 'Double, double, toil and trouble...', which causes him to hallucinate. He dreams himself as King. He dreams himself as unbeatable in battle. He also dreams several other images which he does not understand, or prefers not to accept, at the time. When he wakes, he is hung-over and the once warm witches' cavern is a cold, damp cave again.

The witches allow Macbeth to play on his own ambitions and these weaken him to his wife's apparently more powerful ambition. However, just as she is about to murder Duncan, because Macbeth will not, she discovers that he looks too much like her father. Despite her apparent ruthlessness – 'Stop up the access and passage to remorse' – she cannot complete her own plan.

Cutaway 2
Take 1

Lady Macbeth says that she has 'given suck' but there is no evidence of children in either the original play text or any of the filmed translations.

From your knowledge of the historical period, suggest how Lady Macbeth may have had children but has none now.

Consider the effect of the possible loss of her children on Lady Macbeth's ambitions for her husband.

Macbeth recognises that killing the King is a 'deed of dreadful note' and when he has been pushed into the murder he accepts that 'To know my deed twere best not know myself'. His best friend Banquo recognises the changes in his friend when he observes the apparent fulfilment of the witches' prophecies and soliloquises "I fear thou play'dst most foully for't".

Casting and Translation

A comparative viewing of the first eight to ten minutes of both Polanski's and Welles' translations of *Macbeth* establishes that the cast ages are quite different. As the story is about ambition and the role of the wife is central to the achievement of the ambition, different translations become possible with different ages. Similarly, the likely and possible influences on ambition are changed with age. Polanski's Macbeths are quite young (like himself and Sharon Tate perhaps?). In a modern world we might see Macbeth as a Wall Street stockbroker and his wife as a member of the New York social set. It is difficult to see Orson Welles' Macbeth couple in this translation.

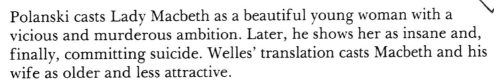

Cutaway 2
Take 2

Polanski casts Lady Macbeth as a beautiful young woman with a vicious and murderous ambition. Later, he shows her as insane and, finally, committing suicide. Welles' translation casts Macbeth and his wife as older and less attractive.

Consider the differences that would have to be made in Polanski's *Macbeth* if Lady Macbeth was neither young nor attractive.

Discuss the effect of casting Lady Macbeth as an unattractive and older woman.

The relative ages of kings and those who would like to be kings, of children as heirs to great power and of acceptable lines of succession depend partly on personality and opportunity but possibly more on historical and cultural period. Shakespeare's *Macbeth*, like many of his plays, is a combination of fact and fiction where the fact is altered to suit the needs of entertainment for an audience familiar with the intrigues of the Elizabethan court.

In Polanski's translation, Duncan is probably above 60, a suitable age for retirement if battles must be fought. His sons are in their twenties when Duncan announces that Malcolm will be his successor as King.

Consider the effect of casting Duncan as a younger King – the same age as Macbeth – with children who are still too young to rule. What effect would this casting change have on our understanding of Macbeth's reaction to the naming of Malcolm as successor?

Lady Macbeth and the Truth

Whether we read the play-text or a film text, our understanding of Lady Macbeth as the power behind the death of Duncan is likely to remain unchanged. What does change is the way we view Lady Macbeth's motivation for her emotional displays and for her various actions.

Polanski's casting of Francesca Annis as Lady Macbeth makes it difficult to dislike her. She is young, attractive, well-groomed and dressed. The camera first shows her at a distance and we hear her pleasant voice more clearly than we see her. But her response to Macbeth's letter and her subsequent actions leading to the murder of Duncan suggest that she is bitter and vicious. This is consistent with the distance Polanski provides and it makes a simple classification of her actions difficult. She seems to be in the background, directing the action rather than taking part.

Lady Macbeth's eventual breakdown and death seem inconsistent with her early strength but we rarely see her in close-up. She delivers significant soliloquies but they are often overheard from a distance – as by the physician. The only clues we have about Lady Macbeth's real nature are inconsistent and incomplete. She is quick to recognise opportunity, both from the letter and from her plan for Duncan; she is ambitious for her husband; she appears to be bitter and ruthless as she expresses her wish to be more like a man, "stop up the access and passage to remorse", and willing to dash out the brains of her child to achieve her purpose, "pluck'd my nipple from his boneless gums, / And dash'd the brains out". On the other hand, she cannot kill Duncan when she has the opportunity because he reminds her of her father and she is ultimately overcome with the blood on her hands: 'Out, damned spot! out, I say'. Before her death we see her at an extreme distance and completely nude – revealed in every detail but too distant to be understood.

The role of Lady Macbeth is never clarified in Polanski's translation. She has power over her husband but it is not sufficient to hold him in control of the throne. She may be wicked, cruel and even responsible for the tragedy but Polanski never allows us close enough to see more than her grace and beauty when she is acting the gracious hostess before the assassination. We might see Lady Macbeth as evil but the King never can.

Cutaway 2
Take 4

Dressed in blue and white, Lady Macbeth wears the colours of the madonna. Discuss the different ways in which Polanski suggests Lady Macbeth's gentleness and loving nature while shifting the appearance of evil intentions to her husband.

Compare your reading of the film with your reading of the relevant scenes in the play; has Polanski created a fair translation of Lord and Lady Macbeth?

We are reminded of the witches' words, "Fair is foul and foul is fair ..." and of Duncan's observation of Cawdor. Nothing is as it appears and since it is not possible to see what people are really thinking trust is a real problem. Shakespeare had already explored this theme more fully in *Richard III*. Polanski suggests it more completely in his presentation of the relationship between Malcolm and Donalbain. The final scene showing Donalbain seeking the witches suggests that he will follow Macbeth's path in seeking to be king in place of his own brother. We cannot foresee the future but Polanski, as director, suggests that it repeats itself.

Cutaway 2
Take 5

Cawdor dies brutally but bravely. Polanski and Tynan provide him with dying words, "Long live the King". Malcolm and Donalbain are confused but Duncan dismisses them with the statement, "There is no art to find the mind's construction in the face". Compare this treatment with Orson Welles' translation of the same sequence. Which is the more powerful sequence? How does Welles' translation assist our understanding of Malcolm and Donalbain in ways which Polanski omits?

"Yon castle hath an pleasant seat"

Writing the screenplay for a film requires two major elements: a clear idea of how the intention of the original text will be translated to the screen; and a careful selection of the original textual elements which are essential to the screen translation.

Most of us have a clear cultural base for picturing a castle. If we come from cultures with strong British literary links, we are probably familiar with the kinds of castles English kings and queens lived in – from the outside at least.

If we come from non-British cultures, we may see castles completely differently. Akiro Kurosawa's Japanese translation of *Macbeth* onto film, *Throne of Blood*, follows the play-text quite accurately but the castles are made of timber. They would not have been out of place in northern Canada a century ago. Castles and fortresses in Pakistan or India are different again, in both shape and size. Some Scottish castles are small; protected homes rather than turreted fortresses. To film the Macbeth Castle, Polanski found an existing castle in Wales.

Stormy Weather

Though Shakespeare's audience would have been satisfied with the description of the birds flying in and out of the turrets of the Macbeth castle, Polanski and Tynan have omitted its description in place of a visual 'reality'. In making this decision, they have taken the opportunity to replace a scene of dialogue with a visual procession. When Duncan first sees the Macbeth Castle, it is bathed in sunlight and looks quite welcoming. As the royal procession advances, clouds gather and as the castle gates are thrown open to welcome the King, rain begins to fall and people scurry for shelter. A fierce storm blows into the festivities of the banquet held in Duncan's honour that evening and the shutters have to be locked to keep out the fury of the storm. It is worthwhile comparing this omission of a complete scene with Welles' treatment of the same scene.

Links between the weather, which was believed to be controlled by the gods, and human events are quite common metaphors in literature. Their linking seems to be quite natural. We enjoy pleasant events in pleasant weather. A picnic in a storm is not likely to create fond memories. The storm over the Macbeth castle sets the atmosphere for the murder. Just before Duncan arrives, we see Lady Macbeth at a distance on the battlements with the sun behind her and her hair flying in the wind. The storm over the witches' cave follows the execution of the opposing army at the beginning of the story. Macbeth seeks the witches in darkness, and fog has hidden the witches in the Polanski prologue. Later, Macbeth will be crowned in sunlight but it will be the last sunny day to be shown. In the end, Donalbain will repeat Macbeth's visit to the witches in wind and rain.

Cutaway 2
Take 6

From your viewing of the Welles translation, identify the sequences in which weather and natural setting are used to heighten or parallel emotional mood or literal meaning. Compare these with Polanski's treatment and suggest which translation makes the more powerful symbolic use of nature.

Lady Macbeth looks like an Amazon on the battlements as Duncan arrives. Suggest what he might have said to his travelling companions if he had been able to see her. How would this dialogue affect what Duncan might say when he first meets her?

The Crown Sent Spinning

The symbolism of flags, language patterns and costume helps us, as viewers, to read the images we are seeing without the need for dialogue. As a result, film can create meaning without words. The picture may not be worth a thousand words but it tends to reduce the need for words to a minimum. It may even create the possibility for words which could not be used without the images – as with Cawdor's final cry.

When Duncan is killed, his crown is knocked to the floor. The camera sees it spinning across the room. Orderly rule in the kingdom has been destroyed. When Lady Macbeth tells her husband "My hands are of your colour" and "A little water clears us of this deed", she suggests first that they can share the burden of their guilt but then that it is easily washed away and forgotten. Perhaps she foresees her future in the bloodied water we see in the barrel but cannot accept it. Polanski never allows us to see her so clearly as at this point.

Key Shot

Reference to Pontius Pilate washing his hands of responsibility for the trial of Christ is a useful intertextual connection in helping to understand the symbolic gesture.

The symbolism of Macbeth's crowning as King of Scotland while standing on the stone of Scone is still practised. The Stone of Scone is placed under the throne in Westminster Abbey where the King or Queen of England, Scotland, Ireland and Wales is crowned.

Meaning Without Words

The opening and closing scenes from Polanski's *Macbeth* are added to the play-text by the screenwriters. Neither appears in the play-text and yet they each help to shape an interpretation which is not possible from the play-text.

The opening sequence which flows from the fog and returns to the fog suggests that what has happened can keep happening with every tide.

The closing sequence, in which Donalbain is about to visit the same witches' cave where Macbeth hallucinated the events of the play, suggests a return of these events. Just as the tide can reveal the events again and again, Polanski and Tynan suggest that the return is already taking place. The casting of Donalbain as a physical cripple may be suggesting that Macbeth is an emotional cripple, and therefore vulnerable to his wife's twisted ambitions. He is certainly excused from the Banquet where he sees Banquo's ghost at the table on the basis of a recognised illness – probably epilepsy (which Julius Caesar also suffered).

Cutaway 2
Take 7

Using your research of Elizabethan attitudes to illnesses like epilepsy, suggest how Macbeth's vision of Banquo's ghost might have been understood by a Shakespearean audience. Compare this understanding with your own reaction to the appearance of the ghost.

Macbeth sees Banquo as he was murdered but the murderers have not told him what they did. Discuss how this knowledge affects your understanding of the way film is constructed to satisfy your needs as a viewer rather than to portray an accurate image of the events they seem to describe.

Ross and the Minor Characters

Although both Welles and Polanski retain most of the minor characters, they have little to say and tend to act as a chorus which allows us to see how the people around the events are seeing them. To maintain close interest in the story-line, the screenscreenwriterriter tends to focus attention on the major characters. This focus usually leads to a reduction in the number of speaking parts in a film translation.

Polanski extends the role of Ross, however. Ross appears in every important scene. He does not always speak but he always sees what is happening. He takes the chain of office of Cawdor to Macbeth in the beginning to start the tragedy. He allows the assassins into Macduff's castle and confronts Lady Macduff before she is murdered. He then takes the news of their death to Macduff and Siward in England where they are waiting to overthrow Macbeth and return Malcolm to the throne. He becomes a surviving character who has no loyalty, who never seeks to rule but always has power because he is always on the winning side. Shakespeare's plays often feature characters who play small roles in the main storyline but who are successful in retaining their influence at court as rulers change. Casea fulfils a similar role in *Julius Caesar*. As screenwriters, Polanski and Tynan have created Ross as a 'political survivor' and reduced the number of speaking parts in a single action.

Cutaway 2
Take 8

The camera angles and lighting are useful pointers to the roles played by Ross at different points in the Polanski translation. Identify three important scenes in which Ross is a silent witness and compare the way he is lit and the angle he is filmed from in each sequence. Use these findings to suggest how Ross becomes one of the major characters in the screenplay without ever taking a major part in the action.

Consider how the role of Ross in Polanski's film establishes the power of the director to construct interpretations of events without changing the play-text.

Explore possible reasons for Polanski causing Ross's helmet to be knocked off during the final fight between Macduff and Macbeth. What does it suggest about Ross's future?

Further Opportunities for Discussion

Many of the famous sayings from Shakespearean plays can be found in *Macbeth* but not all of them are accurately used. Identify as many recognisable quotations as you can from the play-text and compare them with the way they are normally used: eg "Lead on Macduff" is actually "Lay on Macduff". What others can you find?

One of the weakest scenes in the Polanski translation contains one of the most famous quotes from the play-text, "Is this a dagger I see before me ...".

How would you change the filming of the scene to strengthen it?

Many of Shakespeare's play-texts contain a philosophical speech suggesting the importance of the events being played on the stage. Often these speeches refer to the stage itself. "All the world's a stage ..." is one example. In *Macbeth*, the play-text includes the lines, "Life's but a walking shadow ... It is a tale/Told by an idiot, full of sound and fury,/Signifying nothing". Suggest how the inclusion of this speech supports the addition of the opening and closing scenes in the Polanski film.

Films exert control over the viewers' opportunities to interpret what the director has constructed. By reference to specific shots, describe how, through distance and angle, the camera marks the rise and fall of Macbeth from the opening sequences in the story to the close.

Director's Cut

In your examination of one or both films, what have you learnt of the director's mind at work, of direction as an art form?

Olivier's *Richard III*.
Laurence Olivier as Richard III and
Ralph Richardson as Gloucester

NEIL ARMFIELD'S *TWELFTH NIGHT* IN MODERN DRESS

John Woods as Sir Toby Belch

Kerry Walker as Feste

Peter Cummins as Malvolio

Section 2
Narration

Chapter 3:
"Once Upon A Time"

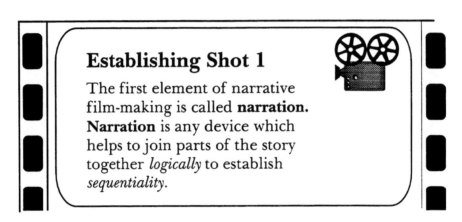

Establishing Shot 1

The first element of narrative film-making is called **narration.** **Narration** is any device which helps to join parts of the story together *logically* to establish *sequentiality*.

Understanding the way film is constructed is similar to understanding the way a novel or a play is constructed. We can use similar words to describe what is happening.

In most western countries influenced by American films, the construction of a film (including the news and documentary programs) is based on four fundamental elements: narration, sequentiality, spatial relationships and closure. These are the same elements we use when we write a *narrative* story.

A narrator is a storyteller whose role is often to introduce or join together events which do not happen immediately after each other or in the same place or at convenient time intervals. Like the newsreader who provides a commentary for images from an on-site broadcast, the narrator tells us how to 'read', how to interpret, what we are seeing. In Greek theatre the role of the narrator was performed by the *chorus* and, in some of Shakespeare's play-texts, the narrator is titled *chorus* (eg *Henry V*).

Some Shakespearean plays, such as *Troilus and Cressida*, begin with a spoken prologue which sets the scene; *Julius Caesar* opens with a group of townspeople who explain that the play opens on a public holiday. In *Othello*, Shakespeare uses Iago's wife, Emilia, to move between Desdemona, Iago and Michael Cassio. In filming *Macbeth*, Polanski uses Ross to provide logical sequence as we move with a known character between unrelated scenes. Ross sees the murder of Banquo and of Lady Macduff but he also comes to the English camp and tells these events to Siward and Macduff.

Narration on film has the same purpose as literary narration. We are familiar with a number of narrative devices which are used to link scenes. Polanski uses fog to change from the opening scene with witches to the battlefield with the king, sunsets come before dawn, *zooming* towards a door or a window suggests that the next scene will be inside.

Key Shot

Zoom – The camera lens is adjusted to make the subject appear to move towards (Zoom In) or away (Zoom Out) from the camera.

A more literary film device is the use of voice from one scene to carry over into the next or to describe one event while we watch another.

Key Shot

Voice-over: Narration or dialogue continues from one shot to the next.

Branagh uses this *voice-over* technique as he delivers the 'Once more into the breach' speech in *Henry V* while we watch his soldiers' faces change from fear and defeat to bravery again. Often, however, the voice-over is performed by someone removed in time or place from a scene, or as a lead-in to it.

The camera only allows us to see characters and events as the film-maker wants them to be seen. The *camera angle* provides another key element in the grammar we need to read film. In more familiar terms, it focuses us on a single *point of view*.

Key Shot

Camera Angle: The angle from which the camera is 'looking at' the subject.

We are used to *looking up* to heroes and *looking down* on people who are weak or threatened. Looking down with a *downshot* can be used to show us people in danger.

Key Shot

Down Shot: The camera is tilted to look down at the subject.

A *long shot* with a *telephoto lens* across a room full of people can tell us that someone is in love with the character at the other end of the long shot. Lucentio falls in love with Bianca at first sight from a distance in Zeffirelli's *Taming of the Shrew*. Tybalt glimpses the hated Romeo across a room full of partying people in Luhrmann's *Romeo and Juliet*. The long shot of Lady Macbeth combing her hair at her dressing table prevents us from coming close enough to understand her state of mind. Her apparent isolation may suggest her detachment from human values or feeling. Polanski leaves the reading of the scene to us as readers and, in the process, opens options for interpretation which may not be available in other translations.

Establishing Shot 2

Power relationships are established on stage with voice, costume and position. In film, they are also established by using camera angles to create a **point of view**

Director's Cut 1

In the balcony scene from *Romeo and Juliet*, Juliet is at home in her room upstairs while Romeo is outside on ground level. The director, Baz Luhrmann, brings Romeo into the garden and then brings Juliet outside to join him. Discuss how the power relationship between the two lovers is established by the director's decision to bring Juliet into the garden on the same level as Romeo instead of having her on the balcony with Romeo needing to climb up from below.

Music plays an important part in most films. It is used to establish historical time, to set mood and to create suspense. It may also be used to show the connection between characters or events. Polanski uses a range of music from rock to unaccompanied boy soprano in *Macbeth* while Zeffirelli uses classical orchestral and solo instrumental music in *Hamlet*. The type of music used by film-makers may suit the narrative but it must also suit the audience that the film-maker has in mind when the film is made. Luhrmann's rock-and-rap score is appropriate to the young audience he has directed *Romeo and Juliet* towards; it is also very appropriate for establishing the period in which the film is set.

Cutaway 3
Take 1

Working in a writing team, brainstorm five useful types of music for showing the powerful emotion of jealousy that Othello might feel when he is told that his wife, Desdemona, has been unfaithful with his lieutenant, Michael Cassio. List these briefly.

Decide on the most suitable music to play when Macbeth is told by the three witches that he will be the King. Write a sequence of shots to show Juliet leaving Romeo on the balcony and preparing for bed. Suggest the type of music that would be useful to support the sequence.

Speech (called dialogue in play-texts and film scripts) can be more powerful on film than in literature because there is no need for the vision to stop while we hear what is being said. We know why Mel Gibson is being mean (dialogue) to Ophelia in Zeffirelli's *Hamlet* because we can see (visual) that he knows Claudius and Polonius are spying on him.

Music, images and camera angles can be used together with dialogue to provide information in ways which are not possible in books because of the need of most of us to read along lines one at a time. Even if we skim, the story can only be told in a single sequence.

"There's no art To find the mind's construction in the face" says Duncan in *Macbeth*. But the film-maker's construction is equally difficult to see because the strength of film to demand that we use several senses at the same time makes the medium very powerful. This is one of the important reasons why we need to understand how film and television broadcasts are *constructed* – so that we can keep a critical or curious mind on the story and on how it is being told *while we are 'reading'* the film. Our *critical reading* of a film must be able to match consciously the decisions the film-maker has made at every point in the film if we are to decide whether we agree with the interpretation. Reading critically does not mean that we set out to view the film so that we can criticise it in a negative way. Instead, it means that we watch and listen for the way the story is constructed at the same time as we watch and listen to *enjoy* the story.

Shakespeare's intention to provide entertainment was important. He had to be successful at the Elizabethan box office or his rival production companies would take his audience and he would lose money. The film-maker of the late twentieth century has the same problem. Films that cost $135 million to make need to be very successful to return a profit at the box office. Most Shakespearean films have been modestly budgeted by comparison with the latest blockbusters. Not many people would take the financial risk of translating a Shakespearean play into film unless the film-maker and the stars were well known and popular. Hugh Heffner's decision to finance Roman Polanski's film production of *Macbeth* is a notable exception.

Editing is another way that films are narrated – some people call this *cutting* – or by the French word, *montage*.

A film may be shown to us at the cinema or on the television screen as if the events happened one after the other in order. The reality is much more complicated.

Because films are not filmed in their final order and because actors sometimes make mistakes and because some shots have to be filmed or *shot* again and again, the editor is a most important person in deciding what the finished film will look like.

When the director decides to edit the film, the result is called the *Director's Cut.*

Director's Cut 2

The second cut of Kenneth Branagh's four-hour filming of the play-text of *Hamlet* is less than two hours long. It is worth comparing the two films to consider what Branagh chose as the most important part of the published text.

If a sequence is supposed to be very exciting – like the battle scenes from *Henry V* or the murder scene from *Julius Caesar* – the editor must cut the shots together to help create this effect. Very short shots from different camera angles help to create a fast, exciting effect while long shots with little action might help to make the scene more tense. The car chase sequence from *Bullitt* is an interesting example of short cutting to create fast-paced excitement.

Cutaway 3
Take 2

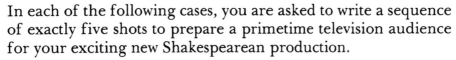

In each of the following cases, you are asked to write a sequence of exactly five shots to prepare a primetime television audience for your exciting new Shakespearean production.

1. Make use of dialogue only with a visual display of characters' heads against a background of fireworks to publicise the scene in which:

    a. Richard III arranges for the death of Lord Buckingham;

    b. Titania falls in love with Puck because she is under a magical spell.

2. Make use of editing only to introduce each of the following:

    a. a mysterious character has arrived who will later be very important to the leading male character;

    b. a group of strangers will change the whole direction of one of the central characters;

    c. someone is coming with bad news.

Discuss the possible uses of music in 1a, 2b. and 2c.

Each of the following is an interesting example of editing for different moods and different audiences:

❖ the slaughter of Lady Macduff and her children in Polanski's *Macbeth*;

❖ the St Crispin's Day speech from *Henry V* by Olivier as compared with Branagh's treatment;

❖ Desdemona's speech to her father about the responsibilities of a daughter from Parker's *Othello* and Capulet's advice to Paris in Zeffirelli's *Romeo and Juliet*.

Each is worthy of close examination to decide how the editor has assisted the film-maker in establishing a particular view of how the event is important in establishing a translation of the director's vision.

Cutaway 3
Take 3

Work in scriptwriting teams of two or three to decide on the camera angles and shot descriptions for three shots in a sequence for a new television serial based on the death of Julius Caesar. Include Brutus, Cassius, Caesar and Mark Antony in at least one of the shots but only Caesar and Brutus in another

Suggest camera angles and possible music for each of the following shots:

❖ Caesar tries to convince the Senate that he is in no danger.

❖ Iago speaks in soliloquy about his hatred for Michael Cassio.

❖ Juliet persuades her nurse to help her meet with Romeo.

❖ King Lear reacts to statements of love from Goneril and Regan.

Chapter 4:
Julius Caesar

Establishing Shot

At least 42 different versions of *Julius Caesar* have been made for film or television presentation. This chapter focuses on the two best known film versions:

❖ directed by Joseph Mankiewicz (1953) starring Marion Brando

❖ directed by Stuart Burge (1969) starring Charlton Heston

Openings

Since the film-maker can presume that the cinema audience has already agreed to travel to the theatre and pay to see the film (it is a *captive audience*), the opening is probably not as important as it would be for a television film – where viewers can switch to another channel if their interest is not captured immediately.

Unlike the television film-maker, the cinema film-maker has an opportunity to set up the play without fear that the audience will 'change channels' from a play that looks boring from its opening scenes.

Cutaway 4
Take 1

View the openings of both the Burge and Mankiewicz films.

Working in script review groups of no more than four people, suggest some of the ways that the opening of the Mankiewicz or the Burge film would need to be altered to capture a television audience in the first few minutes of the production – before the first commercial break – and keep the audience from changing channels.

Historical Setting

Both film translations deviate from the Shakespearean play-texts by opening with quotations from Plutarch. The Mankiewicz film presents the text in a heavy, bold script on the screen. The Burge translation delivers the same text as a voice-over. Consider the reasons that both film directors felt it necessary to provide this historical background but that Shakespeare did not. What would be lost to you as a late twentieth century film reader if these historical notes were omitted from each film?

Opening Scenes

The Burge translation opens with a large bird circling the sky, caterwauling. The camera follows the bird – which turns out to be a vulture – as it settles on an overgrown battle field. An authoritative sounding male voice in funereal tones describes the battle which took place at the site. The relationship between the vulture and the Roman Imperial eagle remains unstated but we may begin to make some associations.

Film Credits

The Mankiewicz film presents the film credits as a list in heavy, bold lettering over the background of a cast metal, stylised eagle, the eagle of Imperial Rome, but the Burge translation uses the backdrop of a triumphal procession through the streets of Rome, flashing the actors' names and roles on the screen rather than including them in a continuous list.

Cutaway 4
Take 2

A continuous listing suggests continuities which may not exist in the reading being presented. The flashing of single-name credits suggests an isolation of characters from one another which may be equally misleading.

How do the title sequences of each film translation relate the major players in your reading?

Consider the symbolism created by the juxtaposition of the skull and the chanting voices. What does this suggest about the way we should read the film?

Both the Mankiewicz and Burge films give top billing to Marc Antony (Marlon Brando in the former and Charlton Heston in the latter) listing Brutus (James Mason and Jason Robards respectively) second. Cassius is given third billing in the Mankiewicz film and Caesar in the Burge film, both characters played by John Gielgud.

Cutaway 4
Take 3

In Shakespeare's published play-texts, the "Dramatis Personae" begins by listing Caesar and his family and supporters. The Caesar group is followed by Brutus and his family and supporters, including the conspirators.

Consider the ways in which this order of presentation constructs a translation of the play for the Elizabethan stage which is different from the film credits.

Explore significance in the order of presentation of the casting in each of the films. Is this Antony's play? Brutus's play? Caesar's play?

Music

Music can be used to create atmosphere or to suggest setting. Shakespeare was an Elizabethan Englishman writing a play which he set in Roman times in Italy. The Hollywood approach to music, until the seventies at least, has been to provide grand orchestral accompaniment to apparently historical films including large crowd scenes. Many films have one or several musical themes or signatures (eg, Zeffirelli's *Romeo and Juliet*). Some films are best remembered for a single piece of music (eg, the theme from *Shaft* or the theme from *The Good, the Bad and the Ugly*).

More recent film music tends to use fewer instruments, to use more modern music and to integrate electronic sound effects into the musical score. The result is increasingly intended to create a sound track that stands alone as a commercial music product (eg, the sound track from *The Titanic*). The expense of film-making suggests that this secondary merchandising can be used to cover initial production costs so that box office takings can be seen as profit for shareholders financing the film.

Cutaway 4
Take 4

Discuss the most obvious differences in the use of music between the two films.

Contrast the music used during the screen credits of the Mankiewicz and the Burge translations. Which instruments are featured? Describe the beat of each. Does either seem to you to be "Roman" music? Which musical score sounds more Elizabethan? Which sounds more like a contemporary concert band?

Select several dramatic scenes from one of the films and explain how the selection of instruments and the approach to the scene assists or hinders the development of the dramatic moment which is the focus of the scene.

Use your research notes to discuss how each film uses the musical score to establish setting and to extend the dramatic effect during important scenes.

Endings

The Mankiewicz translation of the play ends on the battlefield, but the Burge translation ends in the evening following the battle with the two successful generals marching between two long lines of their soldiers to Octavius's tent where the body of Brutus lies.

Cutaway 4
Take 5

The Shakespearean script closes with Antony's "This was the noblest Roman of them all...'This was a man'" (68-75) speech followed by Octavius's one-up-manship "Within my tent his bones tonight shall lie..." (78). The Mankiewicz translation reverses the order of the two speakers, leaving Antony the final word, while the Burge translation simply omits Octavius's final speech.

If you were the director, which order would you use? Why? Would you include Octavius's final speech or would you cut it? Why? What else might you do? Why?

Omissions

You have probably noticed that cinemas schedule films in two-hour slots and you may be aware that both the Mankiewicz (121 minutes) and the Burge (117 minutes) translations of the play omit a good deal of Shakespeare's play-text. At 2450 lines, *Julius Caesar* is one of Shakespeare's shorter plays (compare *Hamlet* at 3762 lines or *Richard III* at 3600). Yet, the longer plays and the shorter ones generally have close to the same running time in the cinema. One indication of what is missing from *Julius Caesar* is found by comparing the Mankiewicz and Burge films with the Wise translation which is basically a film of the complete stage play, running 180 minutes. Another is to compare the films with a published play-text.

The decision to add or cut from an established play-text is dictated, in part, by the advantages and disadvantages presented by translation to the film medium itself (whether in colour or black and white, silent or sound).

Cutaway 4
Take 6

A good translation makes consistent choices within a chosen cultural context. View the endings of both the Burge and the Mankiewicz films in detail. Note the relative positions of the important characters, the way the camera views them and the detail of the settings in each translation. Consider the strengths and weakness of each.

Is each ending true to the director's vision in the other scenes of the film? Which ending do you prefer?

Design an ending that includes the body of Cassius.

A more significant consideration is the film-maker's intention in producing the play-text as a film. To be a commercial success, the film translation must convert to cinema attendance, to box office success. To achieve this success, it must pass the first principle of any Shakespearean performance: it must be entertaining. The second principle of any film is that it should make sense; that is, it must have a coherent plot with credible characters involved in action which is sufficiently well explained for us, as film readers, to become involved with, and feel some sympathy for, the characters.

Director's Cut 1

Act I.ii is a long scene (322 lines) which reveals a good deal about Brutus and Cassius through their conversations. Burge omits a significant number of Brutus's lines (37-50; 63-65; 83-89; 162-67; 303-306) and an even larger number of Cassius's lines (54-58; 66-78; 90-92; 100-115; 153; 156-61; 179-81; 297-302; 308-320). Although some of these omissions are a dozen lines or more, most are small cuts of five lines or fewer, suggesting that the director cut the play carefully and judiciously.

❖ Are there aspects of Brutus's and Cassius's characters which are lost through cutting these lines?

❖ What might the audience learn about Brutus's ego or the relationship between Brutus and Cassius in these lines that helps to understand later developments in the play?

❖ What is gained by the omission of these lines?

❖ Mankiewicz, on the other hand, cuts very few of these lines (48-50; 74-76; 83; 112-115; 133-34; 156-57; 215; 262-67; 299) Compare the Mankiewicz and Burge films (Scene ii) for both the information the audience gains and the pace of the films.

❖ Do you find that the Mankiewicz film drags during any of the lines that Burge omits?

The principles of film translation create tension for some Shakespearean play-text scholars who are, occasionally, inclined to treat the text as more important, from a literary viewpoint, than its meaningful translation to a reading audience. In this view, the printed text, in an apparently original form, is seen as a piece of literature which is complete in itself. The role of the text as a script for action is not seen to be as important.

If the literary view is disregarded in favour of the view that Shakespeare was intended to be performed as an entertainment, the consideration of cutting or adding dialogue to establish a meaningful translation becomes a case for making decisions which will vary among individuals, across generations and across cultures. The range of translations included in this book shows how individual the decisions can be. Choices may depend on the country of origin of the film, the choice of screenwriters, the reputation of the actors, the intention of the director or even the opinion of the producers who are providing the money for the film. Most of these possibilities are explored with humour in the film *Shakespeare in Love*.

Cutaway 4
Take 7

In the following activities, you are asked to compare cuts made to the published play-texts by Mankiewicz and by Burge and to comment on the consequences of omitting lines and scenes.

Act I.i: Mankiewicz cuts about one-third of the first scene and Burge cuts over half of it. Both omit lines 15 to 19, banter between the officers and the saucy cobbler, and both omit parts of Flavius's speeches (lines 56-60 and lines 68-71). Examine these lines to see what is lost by their omission. Drama frequently contains redundant parts to make certain that the audience gets the playwright's message.

❖ What decisions have been made by the film-makers which allow them to delete the lines omitted here, either because they are redundant, or because they alter the focus in some way?

In Act II.iv, both the Mankiewicz and the Burge translations omit the scene with Portia, her servant boy, and the Soothsayer completely.

❖ What information does the scene provide?

❖ What is lost or gained through the omission of this scene?

❖ Consider how the scene might contribute to the pacing of each film and then suggest why each director or screenwriter may have omitted it.

The Burge translation omits Act III.i, pp124-48 where Antony's servant brings a message from Antony to the conspirators. The Mankiewicz translation keeps it word-for-word.

❖ What does this scene reveal about the judgments of Brutus, Antony, and Cassius?

❖ If you were directing a film translation of the play-text, would you include or omit this scene?

In Act IV.i, the triumvirate – Antony, Octavius, and Lepidus – displays its evil side by making a hit list of its perceived enemies who must die (including a nephew and a brother), by acknowledging that it intends to subvert Caesar's will, by Antony's disparagement of Lepidus, and by petty quarrels between Antony and Octavius.

The Burge translation omits lines 7-27 and 31-47, rearranging Octavius's final speech.

Mankiewicz, on the other hand, retains all of the scene except for Antony's vitriolic comments about Lepidus (lines 31-40).

❖ Compare the audience's perception of Antony's character in the two productions. Which production retains more of the noble Antony who defended his late friend Caesar at the Forum?

❖ If you directed a film translation of the play-text, which picture of Antony would you wish to present?

Additions to the Text

Both Mankiewicz and Burge add to Shakespeare's script at the beginning of Act II.ii. Mankiewicz shows Calpurnia waking from a dream, crying "Help, ho, they murder Caesar" three times, lines which were reported by Caesar in the play-text. Burge, on the other hand, adds even more, presenting a *montage* of images and voice-overs, incorporating words and phrases from Caesar's report of Calpurnia's dream – presented later in the scene (lines 76-81) – and Artemidorus's written "schedule" at the beginning of Act II.iii.

Key Shot – Montage

From French, literally 'cutting'. The editing together of a number of otherwise disconnected elements to create a meaningful, and often more powerful, whole.

Cutaway 4
Take 8

Examine Burge's Dream scene in detail. Is it an effective sequence in the film? If you were directing the film, would you include Burge's scene, would you stick to the Shakespearean script or would you try another approach?

The Assassination and the Funeral

Two of the most powerful scenes in the play are the assassination and funeral scenes. These are the engines which drive the play through its various conflicts to the final resolution. The Assassination is a most bloody and horrific slaying of the great general and foe of Pompey. The depiction of this scene on film requires careful consideration of choreography (movement of actors) and camera angles. The funeral scene is the pivotal scene in that it concludes with Marc Antony achieving the upper hand over the conspirators. The scene focuses on two magnificent speeches by Brutus and Antony, speeches which are going to determine what happens in the remainder of the play.

The Assassination Scene

1. **Soundtrack:** In the Mankiewicz translation, there is absolute silence except for dialogue during the assassination. This silence contrasts greatly with the cries of liberty after the assassination. In the Burge production, there is an interesting percussive track which adds somehow to the horror of the action. Furthermore the film records the sounds of the daggers entering and leaving Caesar's body. Consider the two approaches in relation to the complete translation they appear in. How important is the background sound in each of these films?

---

2. **Choreography** and the depiction of violence: There is little blood in the Mankiewicz translation. After the other senators stab Caesar, he walks toward Brutus who delivers the final blow, whereupon Caesar crumples to the floor of the Senate. In the Burge translation, Caesar receives some initial stab wounds, walks to Brutus who delivers a blow, but then walks back to the other side of the set where he is set upon and stabbed many times (Plutarch claims that Caesar was stabbed some twenty-three times). Consider the times at which each of these films was made. The 1953 translation, shortly after the Second World War, was a period of economic prosperity and post-war relief from a significant conflict. Burge's 1969 translation followed the assassinations of John F Kennedy and Martin Luther King.

Cutaway 4
Take 9

❖ What does each of these translations say about the cultural sensibilities of the times in which they were filmed?

❖ Which is the more effective?

❖ Explore the ways in which your own cultural context assists you in making your decisions about the presentation of the assassination in each film.

The Funeral Orations

1. **Voice:** Listen to the voices of Marlon Brando and Charlton Heston in the funeral scene. Which voice do you find to be more appealing and persuasive? If you were a citizen of Rome, which Antony do you think you would be more likely to trust – based on voice alone? Upon what would you base your decision?

2. **Camera techniques:** In both translations the speakers are shot from below and the crowd, the Roman citizens, is often shot from above. This tends to create a sense that power rests with the speakers rather than their audience. In the Burge translation, the camera comes close to Heston when he is touching citizens during the first part of the speech. When he is presenting the will, however, he is shot from below and stands by the huge columns, symbols of Imperial Rome. Describe ways that these shots match Marc Antony's intention to persuade the Romans to his viewpoint.

Casting

Casting is a very serious consideration for producers of films based on Shakespearean works. Often London stage actors have been used to lend a feeling of authenticity to the film translations (Olivier, Gielgud, Stewart, Morden). This has frequently been unsuccessful as stage actors do not always feel comfortable with film and appear to present exaggerated performances rather than play the part more naturalistically. Sometimes, however, the casting has been interesting, as with Billy Crystal's grave digger in Branagh's *Hamlet*. At other times it has been disastrous, as with Jack Lemmon in the same film.

The Mankiewicz and Burge productions are strongly cast and we see this particularly in the role of Marc Antony.

As film readers, you may be unfamiliar with either of these actors and this can be an advantage in evaluating their acting as they are less likely to be prejudged on the basis of their names or fame.

Cutaway 4
Take 10

❖ In your opinion, who appears to be the more effective as Brutus, Jason Robards or James Mason?

❖ Who is the more effective Portia?

❖ Note the casting of the older Gielgud as Julius Caesar. Does Gielgud make a more or less effective Caesar than Louis Calhern?

❖ If you were the casting director for a new translation of *Julius Caesar*, whom would you cast in the major roles? Write a justification of your decisions to satisfy your financial advisers.

Effects and Special Effects

Act I.iii opens with lightning and thunder which extend through Act II.ii. For special weather effects, Shakespeare made do with rolling a cannonball across the floor of the upper prop room and setting off a bit of gunpowder – which, as you probably know, led to the fire which burned down the original Globe Theatre in 1613 – but film directors must create a more convincing show.

Put yourself in the position of director of a new film translation of *Julius Caesar*. Decide how you will handle the storm: what intensity of lightning and thunder will you use? Will it be continuous? Will you include the sounds and physical effects of the wind? Will the flames of torches blow and flicker? Will the characters appear to be drenched? Will their hair blow? Will the noise abate when the characters are speaking so that their voices can be heard? How dark will the scene be? (You will find that such issues cannot really be decided in isolation from your general conception of the film.)

Once you have made these decisions, compare your decisions with those used by Mankiewicz and/or Burge. How convincing is the weather in each film? Offer advice to Mankiewicz and/or Burge which will improve the believability of the scene.

Gender Balance

Many of Shakespeare's play-texts suggest that the women are playing significant roles in support of the men who appear to be central (eg, Lady Macbeth). The roles of Portia and Calpurnia (sometimes spelled "Calphurnia") can be usefully explored from the point of view of the strength and dignity of women.

**Cutaway 4
Take 11**

Use the Mankiewicz and Burge film translations to compare Jill Bennett and Greer Garson as Calpurnia and Diana Rigg and Deborah Kerr as Portia. Which Calpurnia or Portia shows the greater strength of character? Which would be more acceptable to those promoting a feminist view? Are there other views which could change the translations to create stronger males by strengthening the females?

Views of the Critics

Film critics frequently make their reputations by writing acerbic, sarcastic observations about actors and productions which are both witty and perceptive. For example, here is Kenneth Rothwell describing Felix Aylmer's Brutus from the "Famous Scenes from Shakespeare, No. 1 (1945)" production:

> *"An apprehensive ectomorph, this Brutus hardly seems capable of plotting the assassination of great Caesar."*

Of the same production, he notes

> *"...the costumes look as though they had seen better days...but then again, I've rarely seen costumes for the Roman history plays that were very inspired."* (Rothwell and Melzer, p115).

The comments are frequently quite cutting and one wonders how actors might respond to such comments as Tom Castner's on Jason Robards' Brutus:

> *"Robards appears to be receiving his lines by concealed radio transmitter, and delivering them as part of the responsive reading in a Sunday sermon."* (Rothwell and Melzer, p121).

**Cutaway 4
Take 12**

Speculate on Robards' private response to such biting criticism.
View the movie and write a positive review of Robards' Brutus. Locate a biting movie review and write a review of the review.

McMurtry describes James Mason's Brutus as

> *deliberate, meditative, his eyes like great dark pools; he is convinced of his own nobility and thus convinces others. Meeting for the first time with the conspirators (II.i), he is calm and matter-of-fact rather than imperative, and step-by-step he takes the leadership away from Cassius, advising, among other things, that Marc Antony not be killed along with Caesar. The disastrous results of this and other of Brutus' advice seems to be noticed by nobody in the film, with the exception of the increasingly distressed Cassius. Sometimes, so great is Mason's hypnotic power, they are noticed by nobody in the audience either.* (McMurtry, 1994: 87)

The role of the film critic in reviewing the director's achievement and the actor's performance seems to be acceptable. It is more difficult to see how the critic's opinion of the audience can assist us as film readers in understanding or appreciating the film. McMurtry's criticism of the audience, however, suggests that she expects film readers to be able to separate their personal involvement with the film from their critical reading of the film.

Cutaway 4
Take 13

Choose any major character, other than Brutus, from the film (eg, Caesar, Cassius, Marc Antony) and use McMurtry's review as a model to write your own interpretative review of the actor's suitability for the role.

Consider whether it is the role of the film critic to comment on audience response and suggest guidelines for such a commentary.

Camera Technique

The unusual profile shots of Brutus (James Mason) and Cassius (John Gielgud) in the Mankiewicz translation are similar to the images we can see on Roman coins of the period. Consider whether Mankiewicz and his cinematographer had a purpose for shooting in this manner. How do such camera angles add an intended atmosphere to the film? Would these shots have any bearing upon the casting?

Setting

The film translations of historical dramas whether from the meta-narrative of the history books or from playwrights such as William Shakespeare, have tended to be large screen epics featuring casts of thousands of extras overwhelming the screen with their sheer numbers. Often these films were filled with high tower shots panning great armies marching or refugees being driven from their homes. This tradition of film-making goes back to the earliest days of movie film-making. The advent of the wide screen and seventy millimetre film, however, literally widened the possibilities with epics such as *Ben Hur* and *Spartacus*.

Today the epic's technological offspring are generally special effects films such as *Titanic*. *Julius Caesar* contains many of the components which would render it

Cutaway 4
Take 14

Examine a clip from a film such as *Ben Hur* or *Cleopatra*, which featured Elizabeth Taylor and Richard Burton many years before they starred in *The Taming of the Shrew*.

❖ **Camera Techniques:** How does the length of camera shot affect the epic aspect of the film? What kind of a perspective of Rome does the viewer get? Are the buildings shot from a distance or from fairly close? Notice the size of the columns. How do they compare with those next to Heston during the funeral scene. What is the effect of having these great columns next to the character delivering a powerful oration to the citizens of Rome?

❖ **Realism:** Comment on the authenticity of the battle scenes in each film translation of Julius Caesar. How do they compare with similar scenes from *Ben Hur* or *Cleopatra*?

a film epic. It has the grandeur of Imperial Rome and the battle scenes which were a part of almost all epic films. Look at the *Julius Caesar* productions in terms of scale. If the classic film epics included high, wide panoramic shots of thousands and lavish sets and costumes, how does *Julius Caesar* hold up against these types of films?

Parody

Some years ago, the American situation comedy *Moonlighting* did an episode based on *The Taming of the Shrew*. Interestingly, there was strong audience reaction to the episode. In the 1950s, the Canadian comedy team, Wayne and Schuster, shot a parody of *Julius Caesar* for the Canadian Broadcasting Corporation. This parody was also aired on the popular Ed Sullivan show "Toast of the Town", nationally televised in the United States.

Productions

In *Shakespeare on Screen*. Rothwell and Melzer list 42 films made between 1907 and 1987 from the play-texts of *Julius Caesar*. However, only one of these (Wise's 1978 BBC Television translation; 180 minutes long) includes most of the Shakespearean script. Eight of the films, mostly shot before 1912, were 10 minutes or less; the earliest feature-length sound film was shot in 1938 for BBC Television and 17 of the other films were also television productions, either in the United Kingdom or in the United States. Ten of the films were produced specifically for schools, generally short features dealing with theme, atmosphere and specific scenes. A range of alternative treatments is also available: a Black-Hispanic production shot at the New York Film Festival; a comparison of four profiles of Caesar (Caesar's view of himself, Plutarch's report; and plays by Shakespeare and by Shaw); a dress rehearsal of the British National Youth Theatre Company; and a six-minute sketch on the Bill Cosby television show. The earliest film, a 1907 Italian production, depicts Shakespeare writing *Julius Caesar*. If various translations of the play are available, it is worth comparing the directors' and actors' visions in several ways. First, the actors chosen to play a major role and the ways the actors play these roles are revealing.

Director's Cut 2

If Caesar is only "a Mussolini-styled windbag", then the fears of Republican Romans are undercut and the issues are diminished. It is worth applying the same lens to Brutus, Cassius, Marc Antony or Octavius.

- ❖ Are these men powerful enough to argue the affairs of state in the Capitol and to command Roman legions?

- ❖ Are they charismatic?

- ❖ Do they have an aura of command?

- ❖ Do they have strong bodies and powerful voices?

- ❖ Do their eyes 'flash like the glint of steel'?

Is each of these questions answered in the casting and camera angles used to present them on the screen?

Further Questions For Discussion

1. Both Mankiewicz and Burge present the argument between Brutus and Cassius, Act IV.iii, largely uncut. Both, however, cut parts of Brutus's "You have done that which you should be sorry for" speech (lines 66-83), but there are differences. Burge cuts Brutus's line "For I can raise no money by vile means" (72), but Mankiewicz leaves it in.

   ► What is the effect of omitting the line?

   ► Decide whether you think that Jason Robards' Brutus (Burge) would have a less difficult time saying the line than James Mason's Brutus.

   ► In which ways would the line detract from the credibility of the Brutus that Mason portrays?

2. Camera techniques: There is more movement by the camera in the Burge production than in the Mankiewicz production. What effect does this camera activity create? An interesting technique employed in this translation is to have the audience see Brutus through the dying eyes of Caesar and, therefore, shift the narrative point of view. Why do you think this was done and how effective is it?

3. The Mankiewicz production is in black and white. Does this create any problems for you as a film reader? How does the use of black and white affect the setting (light and shadow for instance)?

4. What is the central purpose of the costuming in each film. What problems in costuming are evident in the black and white film?

5. The recording of the Canadian comedy duo, Wayne and Schuster, *Rinse the Blood Off My Toga*, is probably the funniest parody on *Julius Caesar*. It tells the story of how a Roman Private Detective discovers who killed 'Big Julie'. How is the bloodstained toga used effectively in the Burge translation?

6. When you have completed your viewing of both the Mankiewicz and the Burge productions, rate the films on at least five of the points you believe movie critics might use to judge each film (eg, acting, cinematography, costumes, sets, sound tracks, film editing, pace, interest). On the basis of your ratings, which film appears to be the better production? Do your ratings calculations match with your personal opinion of the film?
   Which of the critical qualities you have used do you believe the general public uses to judge a movie?

   ► Develop a list of film qualities that seem to be very important for establishing public reaction to a film and rate the films on these qualities.

   ► Use your judgments to predict how well the films did at the box office and then compare your predictions with film awards (Academy Awards, Genie Awards, Cannes Awards), with critical reviews, and with box office film earnings (all of this information is available on the internet).

Chapter 5:
Twelfth Night

Establishing Shot

No director wants to be associated with a production that is simply a carbon copy of previous productions. This is particularly so in the case of Shakespeare, where it is likely that a good proportion of the audience will have seen a particular play before. Hence there is often a striving for novelty, occasionally with incongruous results: a recent Australian production of *King Lear*, for example, introduced popular songs like "My Heart Belongs to Daddy" and had the Fool dressed as Shirley Temple.

Without going to such extremes, a feeling of freshness can be created simply by changing the period in which the play is set. Such a change also underlines Shakespeare's universality: relatively few, if any, of Shakespeare's plays do not permit the director such freedom.

Four film versions of *Twelfth Night* are readily available on video, two of which were adapted from stage productions:

1980: Petruchio BBC/Time-Life Television version. Director: John Gorrie

1986: Director: Neil Armfield (Australian production in modern setting; distribution rights held by Australian Film Institute.)

1988: Renaissance Theatre Company. Directors: Kenneth Branagh and Paul Kafno

1996: Director: Trevor Nunn (British production).

The BBC *Twelfth Night* was one of the few in that project to win general praise. Neil Armfield transferred his highly successful stage production to film so successfully that it won the accolade of 'notable production' in a British publication, *Shakespeare in Performance* (Parsons and Mason, 1995), as did Kenneth Branagh's and Paul Kafno's Renaissance Theatre Company production. On the other hand, the Trevor Nunn film, a big budget production, and the only substantial translation of the play-text into the film medium, received mixed reviews.

Director's Cut 1

Begin at the beginning? Shakespeare's play-text opens at Orsino's court, and we learn of his love for Olivia. The second scene shows Viola and the Sea Captain, who have struggled ashore from the wreck. Over the years, many stage directors have reversed these scenes, and in the film versions we are discussing in this chapter, two directors have taken the same path. What are the arguments for and against this change?

Setting

Each of the films/videos under discussion shifts the period of the play from Elizabethan times: the BBC version adopts Stuart dress, and much of the action takes place in two Jacobean mansions; the Neil Armfield version has a modern setting (a Sydney seaside suburb or a Great Barrier Reef island); and both Kenneth Branagh/Paul Kafno and Trevor Nunn have chosen the 19th century.

Time and Space

The action of the play covers a period of approximately a week. This raises the question, allied to that of setting, of whether a particular season of the year should be signalled. A production which gives weight to the play's title, for example, might well choose a winter setting (Twelfth Night was the twelfth after Christmas and the final night for festivities). On the other hand, a director wishing to create a 'sunny' comedy might choose spring or summer. Which season do you think best fits the mood of the play?

Both the Armfield and Branagh/Kafno versions, presumably because of financial considerations, have what are basically stage sets; in the BBC version, the camera moves more freely, and in Trevor Nunn's cinema version, we are presented with a wide variety of indoor and outdoor settings.

Cutaway 5
Take 1

In your group, view at least two of the four versions.
Then consider the following questions:

❖ Is anything lost by moving the time forward from Elizabethan times?

❖ Would it be credible to develop a translation set in a futuristic setting?

❖ Dress often signals social status. In the versions you have read, what is signalled about Maria's status in Olivia's household?

❖ In reading the Branagh/Kafno and Nunn versions, what differences do you notice in the costuming? Do these differences affect your response?

Cutaway 5
Take 2

Do you find the severely limited settings of the Armfield and Branagh/Kafno versions constricting to you as a reader? Does it worry you that, in the words of one reviewer, in the Branagh/Kafno translation Olivia and Orsino appear to live on opposite sides of a cemetery? (Note the surrealistic touch in this set.) Are there any advantages springing from such restricted settings?

Cinema or Television

Of the four versions under consideration, only the Trevor Nunn production was specifically designed with the large screen in mind; all the others were prepared for television or video player. In your group, discuss the different demands and possibilities of each medium.

One obvious difference, of course, is the greater use of close-ups in television. Compare the Trevor Nunn version with one of the others in this regard.

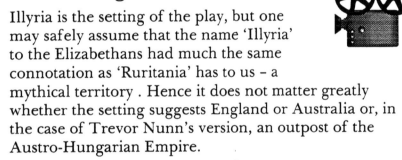

Establishing Shot 2

Illyria is the setting of the play, but one may safely assume that the name 'Illyria' to the Elizabethans had much the same connotation as 'Ruritania' has to us – a mythical territory . Hence it does not matter greatly whether the setting suggests England or Australia or, in the case of Trevor Nunn's version, an outpost of the Austro-Hungarian Empire.

The original Illyricum was the name given by the Romans to the territory on the eastern coast of the Adriatic Sea, in other words, modern Bosnia and Albania. In the late 19th century, most of this territory was indeed part of the Austro-Hungarian Empire.

Willing Suspension of Disbelief

Viola and Sebastian are twins. On stage, the two actors are dressed similarly, and that is generally considered sufficient for the audience to suspend disbelief. But is it sufficient on film, since film audiences have long been fed on 'realism'? Compare Neil Armfield's solution (Gillian Jones plays both roles) with the decisions of the other directors to cast actors with some facial similarity and similar hair styles. In the Branagh/Kafno version, Frances Barber's Viola and Christopher Hollis's Sebastian certainly resemble each other in looks, but is it likely to worry film audiences fed on realism that Olivia does not notice that 'Cesario' has grown in the space of a few hours? The technical flexibility of film allows the solution adopted by Armfield. Why, then, didn't the other directors adopt the same strategem? How important are these decisions in establishing a credible translation of the play-text from an Elizabethan stage to a modern television or cinema screen?

Cutaway 5
Take 3

In what ways are the audiences of stage plays educated to suspend belief and not demand absolute realism? Alternatively, in what ways are film audiences 'educated' in the opposite direction? Is the average film truly realistic?

Sexuality in Illyricum

Inevitably, in a play where there is a boy playing a girl playing a boy (remember that in Shakespeare's time female roles were taken by boys) notions of gender – homosexuality, androgyny – lurk not too far below the surface. Further, there is the fondness of Orsino for 'Cesario' and the attachment of Antonio to Sebastian, a feeling so great that he ventures into the Count's territory at great risk to himself. This potential for confusion has recently been illustrated again in the film *Shakespeare in Love*.

These apparently dramatic devices involving twins and females in male roles to complicate the plot also offer considerable scope for comedy and the case of mistaken identity is used in several of Shakespeare's comedy play-texts. It is used equally effectively to promote the view that an intelligent woman is quite capable of outwitting men – even in such a difficult setting as the courthouse (as Portia does in *Merchant of Venice* when she fools the judges and outwits Shylock).

Director's Cut 2

One of the decisions a director must make is whether to ignore or play down suggestions of homosexual feeling or to emphasise them. Neil Armfield took the latter course: Orsino and Cesario are shown sharing a large swinging hammock, to the surprise of the courtiers.

Consider one of the other film versions. Are questions of gender given any prominence beyond the basic notion of disguise?

Stage productions in the twentieth century have increasingly made Antonio's attachment to Sebastian explicitly homosexual; in the 1930s Denise Coffey went a stage further by drawing attention to the fact that there are no lines in the play ordering his release. At the end of her production the lovers are so wrapped up in themselves that they forget about him, and he is led off by guards, presumably to execution.

Clowns, Fools, Fun and Melancholy

The grim note struck at the end of Coffey's production reminds us that perhaps the biggest decision confronting the director is making up his/her mind about the tone to be established in any translation of a play-text to performance. The key characters in the establishment of that tone in *Twelfth Night* are Feste and Malvolio.

Feste, in these four versions, is played by Trevor Peacock (BBC), Ben Kingsley (Nunn), Anton Lesser (Branagh/Kafno), and Kerry Walker (Armfield). None of the actors plays the role for laughs. The nearest to a comic figure is Trevor Peacock who conveys the sense that as a clown he is long past his prime. The others are all of a melancholic temperament, an interpretation supported by the gloomy songs that Feste sings.

Cutaway 5
Take 4

It can be argued that a Feste who is genuinely funny would do violence to the play. Given the songs Feste sings and the lines he delivers, and from your reading of the films and televised play-texts available, is this a reasonable argument?

All four Festes are at various points of middle age. Is a young Feste a possibility?

Some productions have suggested that Feste harbours a passion either for Maria or for Olivia. Do you find such a suggestion in any of the film versions? Would you, as director, see any point in conveying such an impression?

The Comic Characters

One of the criticisms of Trevor Nunn's *Twelfth Night* is that Sir Toby Belch (Mel Smith) and Sir Andrew Aguecheek (Richard E. Grant) fail to raise a laugh. Is this criticism fair? In contrast, John Woods as Sir Toby and Geoffrey Rush as Sir Andrew are certainly comic in the Armfield version. Can you pinpoint the differences in their performances?

Cutaway 5
Take 5

In a comedy as problematic as *Twelfth Night* can be, is it essential that we laugh at Sir Toby and Sir Andrew?

Music

One of the differences between a stage play and a film is that background music generally plays a greater part in the latter. In *Twelfth Night* music plays a major part as one of the three dominant patterns of imagery: images of music alternate with images of the sea and images of love.

Director's Cut 3

Why do film directors require more background music than is generally used in stage plays? How important is background music in creating mood or tone?

In your group, analyse the use of background music, and the prominence and treatment given to Shakespeare's songs, in one of the four film versions.

If you were directing a modern dress film version, what kind of music would you choose?

Malvolio

Some directors have conceived Malvolio as a comic character from the beginning; others see him as a character containing elements of the tragic. If the latter view is emphasised, *Twelfth Night* can become a very dark comedy indeed.

Director's Cut 4

Charles Lamb, discussing the part in one of his essays (*On Some of the Old Actors*), proposed that:

> Malvolio is not essentially ludicrous. He becomes ludicrous but by accident. He is cold, austere, repelling: but dignified, consistent, and, for what appears, rather of an over-stretched morality. Maria describes him as a sort of Puritan; and he might have worn his gold chain with honour in one of old round-head families, in the service of a Lambert, or a Lady Fairfax. But his morality and his manners are misplaced in Illyria. He is opposed to the proper levities of the piece, and falls in the unequal contest. Still his pride, or his gravity…is inherent, and native to the man, not mock or affected, which latter only are the fit objects to excite laughter. His quality is at best unlovely, but neither buffoon nor contemptible. His bearing is lofty, a little above his station, but probably not much above his deserts.

Do any comments about him by other characters in the play support this interpretation?

Donald Sinden, a highly praised Malvolio (John Barton's Royal Shakespeare Company production, 1969), sees Malvolio as essentially a tragic figure. His imprisonment almost sends him mad, and at the end his degradation is so great that "I believe there is but one thing for Malvolio – suicide". (in Brockbank, 1988, p.66).

Which of our four Malvolios comes closest to Lamb's conception of the role? Does any suggest to you that Malvolio's sufferings have made him suicidal?

Cutaway 5
Take 6

No two actors ever give identical performances of the same part, and, as Donald Sinden has pointed out, no performance of a Shakespeare role can ever be considered the definitive one. What differences do you find between the Malvolios of Peter Cummins (Armfield version) and Alec McCowen (BBC), or between Richard Briers (Branagh/Kafno version) and Nigel Hawthorne (Nunn version)? It is worth studying closely the various versions of the letter scene and its follow-up, the scene where Malvolio appears cross-gartered.

Director's Cut 5

You are directing a film of *Twelfth Night*. You are anxious that the bitterness of Malvolio's departure is lightened in some way. Invent some stage business (no additional dialogue!) that will soften this section so that the audience is left feeling that some reconciliation is possible.

Nunn's Film Translation

As the only version conceived solely in terms of the large cinema screen, the Trevor Nunn version differs markedly from the other three. Note, for example, the way in which the character of Malvolio is filled out by having us see him first in his role of supervising Olivia's servants in their various tasks.

Trevor Nunn's use of cutaways, often less prominent in film than television because of the need for multiple filming rather than multiple use of cameras, becomes a feature of his translation. As a result, while the other three versions present the first interview between Olivia and Viola without interruption, Nunn cuts away from the main action to reveal a startled Malvolio and servants as the voice of 'Cesario' is heard shouting "... cry out 'Olivia'!" in the garden. Later, we see a close-up of his reading matter, a magazine called *Amour*! Nunn also makes effective use of flashbacks, as when Viola ponders the meaning of the ring.

The greater freedom of the largescale production has allowed Trevor Nunn to intercut many visual images of the sea. In doing so, he is able to create a translation in which the sea becomes a character in its own right, vindictive, romantic and jealously separating the characters from a future they can only imagine.

The critical practice known as new historicism has focused attention on the cultural context which helped shape Shakespeare's plays in the first place. For example, *The Tempest* was written at a time of great overseas discoveries and hence of experiments in colonisation. A modern production of the play is likely to highlight those elements that reflect issues relating to European colonisation and its effects, issues which still have relevance today. Is Nunn's decision to set the play in the nineteenth century related in any way to such considerations?

Director's Cut 6

Trevor Nunn has not only reversed the scenes, he has also fleshed out the shipwreck scene by having Viola and Sebastian perform a musical 'drag act' for the benefit of the passengers. How do you believe this affects the credibility of his translation of the play-text?

From a technical viewpoint, the interpretations of the four Violas, the quite different Olivias, and the use of black and white film (more or less) for the Orsino sections in the Branagh/Kafno version, all present challenges for the serious film reader.

Further Opportunities for Discussion

Anton Lesser "gives the jester/musician Feste a mysterious rendition. Student audiences label him a "burnout", and he seems a man with a past." (McMurtry, 1994, p229). How do you see Feste?

"Kerry Walker's Feste was ambiguously androgynous, sang beautiful calypso songs in a very sexy voice, and spoke mockingly in a dry or ironic tone. Real menace was projected through the sexual indeterminacy which [she] brought to the role." – Elizabeth Schafer (in Parsons and Mason, 1995, p227). Is this an appropriate interpretation of Feste?

"Ben Kingsley's anti-social clown, Feste, is close to being the star of the show." – Sandra Hall, *Sydney Morning Herald* 23/1/97. Suggest some of the reasons Hall might have had for making the statement. Do you agree with her observation? Is it acceptable that a minor character should be seen as the star of the show?

Section 3: Spatial Relationships

Chapter 6: Where and When?

Establishing Shot 1

The second element of narrative film-making is called **spatial relationship.** Storytelling only makes sense if we know when and where things are happening and how they relate to each other.

In film, we can tell where things are because we can see the scenery and dress of the characters. If a person carries a sword and rides a horse then we will believe that the action is set in the past. If the same person looks and dresses like us then we believe we are in the present.

Sequentiality, narration and *polarisation* are important for us to feel that we are following the story with all of its complications, resolutions and confrontations. To understand the story completely, we must also know when events follow each other in real time, flash back to past times or jump forward to future events.

Key Shot

Flashback: Sequence from the past set into the narrative present.

A *flashback* takes us back in time but we need to be shown or told for how long we have travelled. Sometimes the use of costume helps us. Sometimes the pages of a desk calendar flick past. Sometimes the hands of a clock begin to spin backwards. One way of showing a flashback is to make the pictures move out of focus and then back into focus in another time while music helps us to understand that time was passing. This technique is also sometimes used to show dreams.

The historical positioning of Shakespeare in Elizabethan times is only helpful in making a film of his play-texts if the play is set in that time. However, Shakespeare wrote some plays as histories. Film-makers, like the readers of a novel, must decide on the historical period before they can develop appropriate responses to their reading. In the same way, Shakespeare's fantasies are timeless and many of his comedies were written as present-time texts. Whatever decisions are made about time within a film, the *spatial relationships* must be made clear by the film-maker.

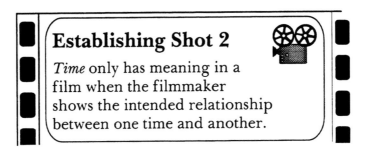

Establishing Shot 2

Time only has meaning in a film when the filmmaker shows the intended relationship between one time and another.

The usual length of a film is about two hours but the time covered by the story in the film can be hours, days or even hundreds of years. The time between one scene and the next varies considerably. If a person is about to fall off a cliff or crash a car into a tree in one scene, the next may show the fall or the crash. When this happens, we talk about a real-time sequence. More often, we do not know whether the next scene is the same day or even the same week, unless the film-maker tells us through narration using dialogue or by use of a clock or calendar.

Although we read film very quickly, we do not always read it accurately during our first viewing because we are trying to connect other information at the same time. For this reason we sometimes lose track of what is happening or where we are in the film. Repeating single images, shots or sequences helps us to keep up with the story.

Repetition also helps us to read the film in the way the film-maker intends us to read. It is harder to read the film critically because we are given information which supports the intended reading constructed by the authors of the film.

Cutaway 6
Take 1

Working in small groups, list some different ways to show that time has been changed in a film. How does each way of showing time change work for the film reader?

In the James Bond film, *Goldfinger*, an atomic bomb is set to explode in Fort Knox in America and make the American gold supply radioactive. While James Bond fights the 'baddies', we are shown the clock timer on the bomb. Although the sequence lasts for several minutes, the timer counts down less than thirty seconds.

Discuss the ways a clock can be used to increase or amplify the feeling of danger in a film. Compare the use of the clock with the use of music to achieve the same effect. Suggest why a clock would be a difficult device to use in a Shakespearean film.

Editing with short cuts, close-ups and rapid changes of camera angle make time seem to move quickly. Editing with longer shots and slower camera movements – like panning – make the time seem longer.

Suggest how the use of slow, peaceful music with long shots may make us feel that time is moving slowly while fast, high pitched music and short cuts can make us feel that things are happening really fast.

Write a brief article for a media magazine explaining how music and editing are used differently to show the passage of time in different film versions of *Romeo and Juliet*.

Establishing Shot 3

Repetition is the retelling or reviewing of parts of the story which have already been told.

Cutaway 6
Take 2

Sometimes the opening of a film shows us the main characters and their relation to each other. It may also show some of the events that will follow.

Work as a media watch team to view the openings or title sequences of several Shakespearean films.

❖ List the character names and relationships between characters which are shown in the short sequences.

❖ Note ways character relationships are developed as the stories are told.

❖ List any examples of repetition of events in the stories.

❖ Discuss the way characters and events are repeated in different stories to give a single reading.

Chapter 7: The Taming of the Shrew

Establishing Shot

Franco Zeffirelli's film translation of *The Taming of the Shrew* with Elizabeth Taylor and Richard Burton is probably even funnier than Sam Taylor's 1929 translation with Mary Pickford and Douglas Fairbanks. Both couples were famous in their times as film stars and for their turbulent romantic lives. Both translations take substantial liberties with the play-text and both result in great entertainment. Shakespeare, we suspect, would have been happy seeing his work drawing so many laughs from the audience. Accepting this need for entertainment, Zeffirelli acknowledges his screen writers and then adds that the dialogue is "by William Shakespeare, without whom they would have been lost for words".

This chapter will focus on the Zeffirelli translation because the Pickford translation is difficult to find. The musical screen translation, *Kiss Me, Kate*, (available on videotape) emphasises the romance but loses the poignancy of the battle between the sexes. The BBC television production starring John Cleese as Petruchio probably provides the best translation of the verbal jousting with Katherine that has been recorded. In this case it is a highly recommended as an access point to the play-text for comparative purposes.

The Opening Scenes

In Zeffirelli's first translation of a Shakespearean play-text (*Romeo and Juliet* followed two years later), Hortensio and Grumio ride down hill through the rain on broken down horses. In the distance lies Padua, unrealistically bathed in golden light with a rainbow arching above – a fairytale town. The music adds to the romantic theme as the pair stop to anticipate the wonderful adventure that is about to unfold for them.

The reality of the main street is crowded, noisy and dirty. The music is drowned by harsh street sounds. Drunkards hang in cages above the street; a whore prepares for her customers. Standing on stilts to increase her height, she adds to the atmosphere. Nothing is as it seems: the romantic is faked, the joy is masking sorrow. The fun is hiding tensions.

Bianca (Natasha Pyne), young, innocent and beautiful, attracts the camera's attention. She does not fit into the surroundings and is quickly shown to be well protected from them.

The shorter 1929 translation, financed by and starring the famous Mary Pickford, omits the establishing sequences and begins with the domestic violence of the traditional puppet show, *Punch and Judy*. Adapted (substantially) and directed by Sam Taylor, the introduction of Pickford as *The Shrew* follows a slow pan to reveal her as the vamp, dressed in a slinky black costume.

Key Shot

In a pan, the camera swivels horizontally to establish relations between objects or actors – or to reveal elements which were previously unseen.

The need to find Katherine a husband before her younger sister, Bianca, can be married is presented in a scene of pure slapstick – even the cat and dog hide from Katherine.

Key Shot – Silent Movie Stars

The comedy of the scene reminds us that Mary Pickford was a star of the silent movies – her rough, uncultivated voice could not match her appearance on screen so she had little success as an actor after sound films were introduced in 1927.

Zeffirelli's introduction of Katherine (Elizabeth Taylor) as an eye peering through a slit in the shutters suggests she is terrifying, malicious and every part the Shrew of the title. Taylor's eyes and her intelligence become the weapons of her dissatisfaction as Katherine – both within the household and during her courtship and marriage.

Key Shot – Stars and Romance

Richard Burton and Elizabeth Taylor were married to each other, twice! Their marriages were reported to be very stormy affairs and Zeffirelli's translation of the play-text may reflect some of the real-life turbulence of the Katherine/ Petruchio courtship and marriage. Whether this is true does not affect our understanding of the interpretation but it does add to the comedy – in a similar way to knowing that Pickford and Douglas Fairbanks were the leading screenlovers of their day.

Culture and the Roles of Women

In the play-text, the arranged marriage of Katherine, the older of two sisters, is a necessary prelude to the marriage of the younger, and apparently more desirable, Bianca – the older must marry first. This socially accepted rule of the Elizabethan period cannot be challenged by any translator of the play-text because it is essential to the ensuing comedy – and its resolution.

The rule, however, is quite common among a wide range of cultures, both historically and into the present day. It seldom leads to comedy, however, as it becomes the source of divisive argument about the succession of family leadership (eg, Henry VIII) and about inheritance (eg, King Lear). *The House of Bernarda Alba* by Garcia Lorca (available on film) presents a modern Spanish tragedy arising from the need for marriage of the older daughter. Amy Tan and Denise Chong present similar tragedies arising within Chinese communities (eg, *The Kitchen God's Wife* – available on film – and *The Concubine's Daughter*).

Apart from the social problems generated by the need to marry the older daughter before the younger, substantial problems are created at personal levels. No sooner is he married than Petruchio takes Katherine from the traditional marriage celebration. He justifies his action with the words, "She is my goods. My chattels ...".

Cutaway 7
Take 1

Petruchio's bath suggests that he is completely careless about his own appearance and hygiene but he has spent considerable time and effort making certain that he looks ridiculous when he arrives at his wedding. Are these two sides of the same character or is one part of the Zeffirelli translation inconsistent with the other?

The concept of women being owned by men has led, and continues to lead, to some barbaric practices aimed at keeping women in 'their places' in the name of family honour. Shakespeare considers the role of the woman in marriage in several plays, particularly *Romeo and Juliet, Taming of the Shrew, Othello* and *Much Ado About Nothing*. In each, he explores the plight of the intelligent woman in an uneven marital relationship.

Without access to divorce and without social support, the woman may be seen as a prisoner, and possibly even a slave, in her marriage. Neither film translation referred to in this chapter explores the issue in depth although Zeffirelli's selection of scenes in both *Romeo and Juliet* and in *Shrew* suggests that he is concerned that it should be discussed. His treatment of Queen Gertrude and Ophelia in *Hamlet* (his third Shakespearean translation to film) continues that discussion.

Cutaway 7
Take 2

Using your research of the Elizabethan period, suggest how widespread the practice of considering wives as goods and chattels may have been. What social and personal gains might be made by the application of such a practice?

By reference to the Ten Commandments in the biblical Book of Kings, consider the strength of religious support for this practice.

How appropriate do you consider the practice of ownership of one person by another in modern society – as a child? as a partner? as an employee?

If you were asked to translate the play onto a modern western university campus, could it be staged credibly? What changes would you make to the play-script and how would you cast the characters?

The Taming of the Shrew presents a highly intelligent woman with an astute wit who is totally unwilling to marry merely for money or position – unlike a number of the wives in *Merry Wives of Windsor*. Katherine is seeking an intellectual companion and her behaviour estranges her from all suitors until Petruchio. His willingness to marry her for the value of her (now substantial) dowry suggests that his manner may be as unacceptable as Katherine's. His wooing is certainly not elegant though it establishes that his wit is equal to Katherine's.

Although the wedding is a deliberately staged comedy, which Zeffirelli might have cut shorter, it signals the beginning of a 'taming' which is generally unacceptable in modern western terms. Seen as a lighter comedy in which two strong minds attempt to gain the ascendancy, it becomes a period of intense comedy. Taylor's translation allows Pickford to overhear Petruchio's plans for her and to thwart them as she pleases. Taylor's Katherine has a tougher role to play.

Cutaway 7
Take 3

In Zeffirelli's translation, the camera seldom comes close to the characters after they arrive at Petruchio's house. Often it looks down at them. Occasionally it looks up at one and down on the other. This helps to create a distance between the characters but it also distances us as film readers. We are forced to stand back, watch and listen to what is happening. Should Katherine be sharing some of the responsibility for the treatment she receives in Petruchio's house?

Further Possibilities for Discussion

❖ The most famous speech in the play-text is Katherine's apparent submission to Petruchio in which she describes a wife's duty to her husband. Mary Pickford delivers this speech standing behind her husband and tips a big wink to her sister Bianca to show that she is *not* 'tamed'. Zeffireli's interpretation shows a much stronger speech in which Katherine explains to both men and women what the duties of a wife should be.

❖ In *Othello*, Desdemona's speech to her father about the differences between duty to a father and duty to a husband expresses similar sentiments but they do not suggest that she is submissive. Consider the speeches from each play and decide whether Zeffirelli's presentation of Katherine shows that she has been 'tamed'.

Key Shot – Intertextuality

All texts may reflect or even assume knowledge of other texts. This feature is called inter-textuality. Sometimes the reflection or reference is very obvious – we often recognise the impossible love match of 'Romeo and Juliet' in modern television dramas – frequently based on mixed-race relationships. But such intertextuality is not only seen in the storylines: the opening scene from Branagh's translation of *Much Ado About Nothing* deliberately reminds film readers of the earlier film *The Magnificent Seven* which, in turn, refers to a Japanese film called *The Seven Samurai.*

Cutaway 7
Take 4

The Taylor/Pickford translation closes with a feast – really the original wedding feast postponed. The music used is the student drinking song from the musical *The Student Prince*. This intertextual reference reminds us that the original intention of the suitors (except Petruchio) was to study at the famous university in Padua.
Suggest how this musical reminder of the opening of the play helps to draw the storyline to an ending in which all of the characters have played significant roles in achieving closure for the production.

Chapter 8:
Othello

Othello was, apart from Shylock, the last major Shakespearean role played by Lawrence Olivier and he was reluctant to do so when asked by the Old Vic Company in 1964. The resulting stage translation of the play-text, directed by Stuart Burge, was presented on film in 1965. The film record of the stage play suggests that Olivier was correct in identifying the problems. Orson Welles' 1951 translation is highly variable in both production and acting. For many film readers, the more recent Parker *Othello* of 1995 is the most accessible translation. This chapter focuses on these three readily available translations, recognising that Burge's stage translation suffers from being a play recorded on film rather than a film translation of the play.

Cutaway 8
Take 1

Olivier's *Othello* is essentially a stage version filmed; Welles' and Parker's are conceived as cinematic versions. Would you expect this to make any difference to your response as you view them?

How do plays and films generally differ from one another?

Othello or *Iago* ? – Translation Problems

Olivier's "actor's sense" of the play is supported by the response of a range of traditional literary critics. Their accounts of *Othello* have varied widely from A C Bradley's "noble Moor undone" by Iago's fiendish plotting to F R Leavis's "fatally flawed individual" who merely needs someone like Iago to accelerate his road to ruin. Either of these extremes has consequences for both Othello and Iago and each oversimplifies the complexity of the characters.

In Bradley's reading, an essentially good and simple soul is destroyed by a cunning, plausible villain. In Leavis's view, Othello's personality becomes more complex. As the drama unfolds, he touches levels he has never previously recognised. Iago, on the other hand, is reduced to little more than a mechanism to bring about the unravelling. Thus, for Leavis, the dramatic challenges of the play-text become more apparent.

Though there is little critical agreement about the nature of either Othello or Iago, their interaction is pivotal to any translation, stage or screen. Both the actors playing these parts must see each of them in the same way so that they can strive for the same goals in the production as a whole. They need to preserve a shifting and tenuous balance between the characters as the play progresses. If they fail, the production is likely to collapse into an emotionally overwrought outburst in which the audience is never sure about what it is appropriate for them to feel. The common view of Othello as too jealous to be credible remains unbalanced in the face of a parallel view that Iago is too evil to be credible.

Recognising this uneasy balance, a great burden falls on the ability of the actor playing Othello to show the complexities of the Moor through the poetry he speaks. On the other hand, it seems, Iago the actor must work in an opposite fashion from the intent of Iago the character. He must always complement and highlight the performance of the Moor to produce a dramatic tension that will be coherent and intelligible to the audience if he is to avoid reducing Othello to an incredible and overly violent pawn. Reviewing the success of the director in maintaining this uneasy balance is one way of evaluating the success of the three films under discussion in this chapter

Cutting and Characterisation

Commercial television stations are often criticised for cutting films to increase the advertising time. This cutting sometimes removes dialogue and even whole scenes which are needed for viewers to understand later scenes. Film-makers are forced to cut the text of Shakespeare's plays to reduce them to practical lengths for the cinema. Because of this necessary loss of text, *Othello* appears to present even greater challenges for the film-maker than it does for the stage producer. While the full resources of the film are available to structure the work and to make dramatic suggestions, these advantages are usually only available at the expense of greater cuts to the play-text than will be necessary on stage.

Cutaway 8
Take 2

Choosing one translation you have seen, explore how the filmmaker compensates for the need to cut the play-text to create the translation.

How are the losses of verse accounted for or replaced in the film?

If you were planning a film version of *Othello* what lines or speeches would you feel it was essential to retain?

Which scenes and speeches would you cut? How would you replace them?

A two and a half hour film translation of *Othello* must consist of considerably fewer of Shakespeare's lines than a comparable stage production. It may also highlight Iago in a dangerous way because there are sequences involving him which must be presented in detail to clarify the plot and carry the action forward for it is Iago who is responsible for initiating the action.

Establishing Shot 2

While Iago acts, Othello mainly reacts but the play is rightly called *Othello*, not *Iago*, and Othello must have the opportunity to be seen fully and sympathetically in those reactions.

Within the filmic conception, Othello must always retain that centrality. At the same time, where Othello's verse is cut, the film-maker must work doubly hard to compensate – with economical suggestions of what the audience should feel about the tragic hero.

Each of the three filmed translations tackles the problem of *Othello* differently. Orson Welles' 1951 version tends to be the most cinematic of the three, the use of the camera to create atmosphere and reveal the story suggesting Welles' earlier success as the creator of *Citizen Kane*. Since the running time is only ninety minutes (the full play-text takes about three and a half hours to perform on stage), it is clear that the script has had to be cut substantially. Whole speeches and scenes are conveyed in a few lines. Welles relies heavily on the art of the film to convey and even substitute for the art of Shakespeare's play-text.

Visions of a Warrior

Welles' translation foregrounds the havoc wrought by Iago and the torture he has brought on himself, to be enforced by the newly elevated Cassio. In the opening scene, the camera is focused on the face of the dead Othello. His body and that of Desdemona are shouldered by pall-bearers and carried solemnly through the crowds to the funereal cadence of a piano. At the same time Iago is dragged through the streets by a chain attached to a collar. He is thrown into an iron cage which is then winched high up against the castle walls while Governor Cassio, sighted among the populace, looks on.

Highlighting the dramatic situation at the end of the play has the effect of emphasising Iago's activity in the play. Audience attention is focused on him as the most prominent living character. The director invites us to ponder his fate. The opening image, however, introduces an enigmatic Othello, impressive, dignified, but about whom large questions remain throughout the film. It is unclear what this imposing man really feels at key moments in the film, such as the temptation scene (III.iii) or the murder scene (V.ii). This lack of clarity becomes a fundamental challenge for us as readers of the translation because we must guess at his motivation. Welles challenges us to judge Othello but establishes the difficulty, perhaps the impossibility, of judging because we do not know – and cannot know – enough about the man. We must consider the translation after we have read it if we are to gain the same sense of closure that we are usually given in the cinema.

It is dramatically and cinematically interesting to see Othello literally putting out the light of the candle when he is about to "put out the light" that is Desdemona. What this actually means to him, however, is never really clear. Perhaps, being a warrior, he sees the two actions as equally necessary. Welles may be suggesting that he is a remote figure, as bewildering for the audience as he is for Desdemona.

Scene-Stealing – The Iago Dilemma

Throughout the Orson Welles' translation, Othello remains regal, imposing and difficult to understand. In contrast, Michael MacLiammoir's mean and skulking Iago is a transparent knave. The vast difference between the two men seems to suggest it should be easy to understand what motivates Othello.

Cutaway 8
Take 3

Working in small groups, identify the features of Othello which suggest that he is: a great warrior general, a romantic hero, an innocent victim of Iago's plotting.

Use these lists to discuss the kind of person you believe Othello must have been.

Does the result of your discussion suggest that he is likely to have been so completely tricked by Iago?

An opposite difficulty arises with the Parker *Othello* of 1995. This, too, is beautifully cinematic in its conception, making good use of localities in Venice (the film opens on the canals) and Cyprus. At around two hours, there is significantly more scope to use more of the original text, but even so, it is heavily cut. Again, much of the cutting takes place at what can be seen as critical moments in Othello's speeches; the motivation for his later, apparently stubbornly self-destructive, actions is lost as the director allows key sections to fall to the cutting room floor. Similarly, it can be argued that the cutting of Desdemona's key speech about a daughter's duty and a wife's duty make it difficult for us to accept her apparent passivity at the climax.

Cutaway 8
Take 4

Use the play-script to discover exactly what has been cut from Othello's speeches in both the Welles and the Parker translations.

Discuss the value of knowing the full text of Othello's speeches.

How does a close knowledge of the original speeches assist in understanding Othello's actions?

Parker's Iago is more prominent than the Iago of either of the other two films. Perhaps because Branagh is the best known of the cast, he is shown as a character with great charisma, a star. The director's difficulty in balancing the production is highlighted in this casting decision. Iago is a highly intelligent, self-controlled and resourceful plotter who thinks of everything. We can easily accept, as we learn from Emilia, that he has wanted the handkerchief for some time. On the other hand, his direct addresses to the audience seem to suggest that he is too brash by far to have been trusted so blindly by the great tactician and general, Othello.

From the early scenes of the film when Iago manipulates three chess pieces representing Othello, Desdemona and Cassio, we are given a clear message that this man is in control of the on-screen action. His ability to be what is needed with Roderigo, Cassio and Othello seems completely confident. At the same time, he frequently stares at the camera after an exchange with another character to deliver a soliloquy which knowingly takes the audience into his confidence and reveals the coldness of his heart and his smug satisfaction in his own cleverness. The selection of dialogue from the play-script makes it easy for us to accept that Iago would resent Othello's preferment of Michael Cassio over him as Lieutenant. It is equally easy for us to accept this as a motive for revenge. The unlikely speeches to the audience confirm his egotism as he breaks out of the film to reach us in our late twentieth century cinema seats – hundreds of years beyond his time – but they should also cause us to ask if this is reasonable in the translation.

Branagh's Iago is reminiscent of Woody Allen's romantic film character in *Purple Rose of Cairo*; he needs to be both within the context of the film as Iago and in the confidence of the audience as the cleverest character in the play – a spurned protagonist requiring audience sympathy. From this viewpoint, it becomes possible to critique both the director's selection of text and Branagh's freedom with the role. James Mason has a more credible role as the narrator in Branagh's *Henry V* but then, Branagh is the star, the chief protagonist in his own translation.

The direction of Branagh's performance highlights the difficulty that Olivier foresaw. The sense that this man is so much cleverer than anyone else in the play helps the viewer to feel that Othello has little chance in dealing with him. The casting of the lesser known Laurence Fishburne in the title role extends that interpretation.

Director's Cut 1

"From his first words in the film, Fishburne gives the impression that he would be more at ease playing the romantic lead in a modern tear jerker than he could ever be representing the imposing bearing of the respected commander of the Venetian forces. He appears to be more at home on the public battlefield than in the minefield of more private emotions."

Discuss this criticism. Is it necessary for Othello to be physically imposing?

Parker presents an Othello with a limited range of responses. Even during the temptation scene he takes rather a long time to become worked up. We might expect a successful general to be used to making decisions quickly. The fact that the scene is presented as a series of vignettes in different settings makes it difficult to follow Parker's intention. What is the film wanting us to feel about Othello?

Director's Cut 2

"It is Othello's physical success that influences the Venetian Senate and underpins his success in wooing Desdemona."

Using the play-script together with the Parker translation, consider Desdemona's speech to her father about her love for Othello. Are the qualities which attract the Venetian State the same as those which attract Desdemona?

It is difficult to discover Parker's intention from Fishburne's performance or his appearance. As we see him, he seems abruptly, rather than suddenly, jealous. He does not respond much to what Iago first tells him and then he is fully convinced. This throws him into a moping distress where he does not appear to know what to do. As readers, we can become confused by his indecision. As viewers, we can more reasonably accept Othello as a seasoned general, a man of action.

Cutaway 8
Take 5

"There is not enough range in the actor's performance and not enough of Othello's poetry remaining to help us understand why Othello would kill his new wife without giving her a chance to explain herself." Is this a fair criticism? What evidence do we have to suggest that Othello might act without apparent reason to kill Desdemona in a fit of jealousy?

Even when Othello finally decides to kill Desdemona, we do not know what he thinks is his reason for doing it.

Cutaway 8
Take 6

Iago, Desdemona and Emilia are in turn allowed to dominate what should be Othello's great scene. At the end we are presented with the tableau of three bodies on the bed and, for some reason, Iago snuggles up to them. Even here, he takes over what is happening! As viewers we must decide whether the director or the actor is in charge of the film.

Discuss possible reasons for the inclusion of Iago on the death bed and compare this scene with the Welles deathbed sequence. What are the major differences? Which is the more convincing for you?

Characterisation may be influenced by casting and casting may not be in the hands of the director. Big name stars and overall budget costs sometimes lead to strange casting decisions. The film translation of *Othello* may be more heavily influenced by the casting than by the screenplay. More importantly, the screenplay may be changed to suit the casting.

Cutaway 8
Take 7

Observe the playing of Cassio, Emilia and Desdemona in a film version of *Othello*. Write a character sketch of each, noting the idiosyncrasies (personal mannerisms) of the actor and how these are employed to create the character.

❖ Does the playing of each character match up with or extend your own reading of these characters?

❖ In what ways does the performance illuminate your sense of the importance of these characters in the play?

❖ To what extent does the interpretation of each of these characters interfere with our attempts to understand Othello's character?

Play-text as Filmed Stage Translation

The longest of the three films is Burge's record of Laurence Olivier as Othello. At 166 minutes, it presents the National Theatre production with most of the original cast and little attempt is made to adapt it for the screen. In effect, it is a filmed stage play though use is made of cinematic techniques such as close-up (not always successfully as Olivier looks very artificially coloured) and camera movement. Interestingly, very little use is made of music. Although the result suffers somewhat as a film, it has advantages in its approach to the play. There is more scope for Othello because more of his lines have been preserved. A very conscious attempt is made to locate the emotional centre of the play within the sufferings of the Moor. At the same time, Frank Findlay's Iago is a substantial figure who seems credible as the cause of Othello's anguish.

Cutaway 8
Take 8

In many productions, Othello is played by an actor in black make-up; Laurence Fishburne in the 1995 *Othello* is a black man.

❖ Does this traditional view have a great impact on the response of the audience to the Moor?

Observe the playing of Othello in each of the translations and decide what effect Othello's racial characteristics have on the film's interpretation of the play.

❖ What difference would it make if Othello were only a little darker in colour than many Europeans (if he were played as an Arab, for example)?

The Voice of Authority

Besides appearing in coal black make-up, Olivier worked on his voice to make it appreciably deeper than normal – perhaps in recognition of the power of Paul Robeson's stage success in the role in the 1930s. Olivier's voice has the effect of increasing his air of authority, as does the fact that he portrays the oldest of the three Othellos under discussion in this chapter. Othello's age, of course, has implications for the casting of Desdemona.

Olivier's Othello is a man who has been a professional soldier all of his life, accustomed to command and to enjoying the loyalty, respect and unquestioning obedience of his subordinates. In the early scenes in Venice, which are much fuller than in either of the other versions, Othello can subdue men with a word or a look. When Brabantio, with his retainers, tries to apprehend him and take him to prison to be later tried for abducting his daughter, Othello takes command of the situation with the famous line

Keep up your bright swords, for the dew will rust them. (I.ii.58)

It is not simply that Othello is fearless nor that he has men with him as willing to do his bidding as Brabantio's, but that he has the habit of command. Brabantio feels some importance as a senator and as one wronged, but Othello has a just sense of the strength of his adversary and his own power in the state. In these public scenes, as also when he acts through Iago's scheming to deprive Cassio of his lieutenancy in Cyprus (II.iii), Othello behaves with the confidence of a man experienced in military and public life. He knows his own value and how it is appreciated. He has clear expectations and demands that they be met. In these scenes, Iago is necessarily the respectful retainer, maintaining a facade that meets Othello's requirements. He is scheming from the beginning but at this stage he can only attempt to undo Othello through others: Roderigo, Brabantio, the Duke. In these areas, however, Othello is impregnable and Iago does not seem able to touch him.

Cutaway 8
Take 9

How does the difference in age between Olivier and Fishburne affect your feelings about their authority as the successful general?

Consider whether the Desdemona from Burge's film could fall in love with Fishburne's Othello. Which of Fishburne's characteristics as Othello are most important in your decision?

The Turning Point

When Iago begins to plant his poisonous insinuations about Desdemona and Cassio, he scores an immediate victory in penetrating Othello's defences. Act III(iii) can be seen as the turning point of the play because the relationship between Othello and Iago changes. Iago's shrewd eye has detected the point of greatest weakness in the general - his inability to understand the range of emotional responses he is feeling in his love for Desdemona. While Othello is a good judge of soldiers, politicians and campaigns, he is basically inexperienced in the subtleties of emotional involvement with women. He has hardly been able to believe his good fortune in capturing the love of Desdemona and he is particularly vulnerable because of the age difference between them. It is not just that she may find Cassio attractive but that he suspects he is ugly and unworthy of her.

Cutaway 8
Take 10

How does the casting of Othello in each of the three films account for the age difference described in the play-script.

It is Othello's emotional uncertainty, his immaturity in serious relationships with women, that Iago is able to play on with such telling effect. Othello's reaction is excessive, almost from the very first of Iago's tentative suggestions. Iago is able to become bolder as Othello swallows the bait until he comes out with his masterstroke, "Oh, beware, my lord, of jealousy!". From this point he has planted all that he wishes into Othello's consciousness. What follows, with the handkerchief and all of the machinations that attend it, proceeds almost inevitably as Othello loses emotional control.

In the first two acts, Othello is the assured old campaigner. He is the macho man, comfortable in command with friends and formidable in command with enemies. In the last three acts, he is transformed - almost into a blithering idiot in some productions. He has uncontrollable emotional outbursts (as when he is reading the letter from Venice, and when he cannot stop calling out as Desdemona is discovered with Cassio and finally strikes her, to the horror of Lodovico who thinks he has gone mad). Olivier's Othello expresses his loss of emotional control as a loss of physical control - a warrior response: he raises his voice, rolls his eyes, rants, strides around the room, rolls around on the floor, has fits. He has become the very antithesis of the cool headed leader we were introduced to at the opening of the play.

Significantly, Burge shows us that the relationship with Iago has also completely altered. From being the trusted ensign with particular functions to perform (but not so trusted as to have been made Lieutenant) Iago has positioned himself at the centre of Othello's emotional life. Othello now relies on Iago for his view of the world, for information about the most important thing in his life, his relationship with his wife. He is shown as powerless to seek verification from the person most able to give it. Maggie Smith's Desdemona intensifies the poignancy of this situation. She is deeply in love with Othello, bound in duty to him but baffled as to why he tests her so relentlessly. Her reaction when he strikes her, "I have not deserved this" is telling. Her restraint makes all the more obvious her husband's lack of it.

Cutaway 8
Take 11

As a trained and successful warrior general, Othello sees the world in simple terms. When things are right he does not act, when they are wrong, he must act without reason or mercy. As a warrior, this is his greatest strength; as a lover, it is his greatest weakness.

After the murder, when he realises the monstrous enormity of Iago's plotting, Othello is on the brink of emotional collapse. The neatly polarised world of his military experience is quite inadequate to his needs. The inadequacy of his manhood has been revealed. In his limited vision of emotional response, there is nothing left for him but suicide – the course he takes.

Director's Cut 3 – Turning points

The turning point of Othello is usually accepted to be the temptation scene in Act III (iii). View the scene as it is presented by Orson Welles, Laurence Olivier and Kenneth Branagh. Note how the scene is produced, the setting, the differences in the script and how the play-script has been amended.

❖ Which do you find the most satisfying presentation?

❖ What suggestions can you make to improve each of the three?

In each translation of the play-script to screenplay, the contrast between the early Othello and the later is quite marked. The result of his personal weaknesses and Iago's ability to perceive and work on them result in the original controlled Othello becoming substantially lost. The difficulty of maintaining a balance between Othello and Iago makes it difficult to avoid melodramatic moments. Othello has to be both the cool public man and the emotional child. The contrast is extreme and, for film, the time is limited.

Cutaway 8
Take 12

View the conclusion of the three films (Act V(ii)). Which do you prefer as a conclusion to Othello? Which most satisfactorily rounds off the thematic preoccupations of the text?

Identifying Translation Problems

The three film translations under discussion help us to identify what might be required for an effective translation of *Othello* from play-text to film. To date, it appears to be one of the most difficult plays to translate – perhaps because it contains two of the most complex characters involved in a plot which seems better suited to the action-epic treatment.

Western film audiences familiar with the Hollywood approach to film-making tend to demand easily understood emotional events because these take least time to develop and resolve. More complex emotional relationships are more common in British and European film treatments. *Othello* seems to contain elements which demand a sophisticated blend of the familiar approaches to allow sufficient dialogue together with sufficient action to create a satisfying translation.

Cutaway 8
Take 13

Plan a film version of *Othello*.

❖ What are the most important features of the play you need to take account of in order that your film may be a success?

❖ What aspects of the relationship between Iago and Othello will you emphasise?

❖ How would you want your actor to interpret the character of Iago?

❖ How will your actor interpret Othello?

Any translation will probably begin with a clear recognition that this is Othello's film, not Iago's. A very daring production might be prepared to minimise Iago's role so as not to cut Othello's, though the result would undoubtedly be a different kind of imbalance. A successful translation will use all that the play-text provides, including Iago, as well as the resources of the film-maker, to probe the elusive complexity of Othello. As with Polanski's *Macbeth*, or the Rosetta stone, the translator's key may lie outside the play in the complexity of loves, hates and jealousies which belong with every man rather than with those Rambo-like characters for whom emotional development is always a crisis of credibility.

Director's Cut 4 – Time and Place

The Welles, Olivier and Branagh films each present *Othello* in a setting which corresponds roughly to that envisaged by Shakespeare.

Consider the potential for translating the play-text to a different time or setting.

❖ What would be the effect if all the cast members were black and Othello white, with suitable adjustments to the text? Might such a change assist in overcoming technical problems with *Othello* or would it create new ones?

Further Opportunities for Discussion

Why has it been so difficult for producers on stage or screen to create a satisfactory version of *Othello*? What advantages might a film-maker have in setting out to do so?

One of the great advantages of a film translation is its ability to use real places and recreate events in full scale. Suggest why Parker may have avoided a recreation of the battle and the storm which take place immediately after Othello's arrival in Cyprus. Discuss the potential value of this sequence of events for showing Othello in his true glory as a worthy general of the State of Venice and a worthy husband for Desdemona.

Observe the delivery of Shakespeare's poetry by both Iago and Othello in sequences from the three film versions of *Othello*. Whose interpretations of the two characters do you prefer? What do the performances show about how Shakespeare's lines may be interpreted by an actor?

> *While Findlay's Iago does what he can to enable Olivier to express both sides of this complex personality, Branagh's Iago leaves little room for Fishburne's Othello to change convincingly. MacLiammoir's Iago presents the third 'extreme' in being too apparently obvious. Leavis's "fatal weakness" in* **Othello** *seems to be an even more crucial weakness in translating the play-script to the screen.*

Use your knowledge of the three filmed translations of *Othello* together with the play-script to discuss Leavis' concept of fatal weakness.

> *Despite the credibility problems created by the coal-black make-up, the excessive posturing and the stage-bound production, Burge's conception of the Othello/Iago interaction is the most interesting of the three translations. The way it changes and develops acknowledges the shifting emotional centre of the play. Its speedy transformation at III(iii) is the key to its success. Nevertheless it is not as satisfying as one could have hoped.*

Discuss the opinion of this critic. Do you agree? The critic identifies obvious weaknesses and complex strengths then shows dissatisfaction. Is this a fair form of criticism? Use your knowledge of film criticism and of the film to write a response to the critic.

Write a critical review of one film of *Othello*. In your review specify the strengths and weaknesses of the film as a film. In addition, point out what it has to offer as an interpretation of *Othello*.

Section 4
Sequentiality

Chapter 9:
...And Then, And Then...

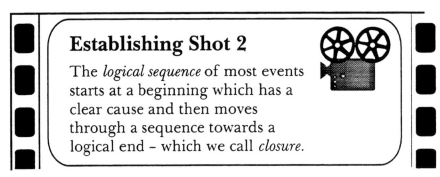

Establishing Shot 1

The third element of narrative film-making is called **sequentiality.** Sequentiality means that things seem to happen in a *logical sequence.*

When Mel Gibson, as Hamlet, looks across his father's coffin to see his mother with her new husband, we know that she has remarried very soon after the King's death. Two events which are separated in time are shown in the same sequence but the time interval is distorted. The play on the stage must show us the two events separately because, as an audience in a theatre, we cannot be seated on stage with Hamlet to see the happily married couple. We accept the sequence of events in the film as believable. Without the play-text in our hands, we remain unaware of the time shift the film-maker has made in joining the two scenes. In the hands of a skillful film-maker, this shift becomes invisible because few of us view the film with the text in our hands.

Establishing Shot 2

The *logical sequence* of most events starts at a beginning which has a clear cause and then moves through a sequence towards a logical end – which we call *closure.*

When events happen out of sequence or do not logically follow each other or result in an *illogical* ending, then we sometimes find the film disjointed and difficult to follow. In extreme cases we might leave the cinema before the end of the film. When the film ends without providing an acceptable ending then we become very aware of our need for loose ends to be tied up, for *closure.* Polanski shows Macbeth 'struck withal' by the predictions of the three witches but he closes the film with Donalbain visiting the witches' cave. The ending suggests that Shakespeare's play will be repeated over and over again, that it is timeless. In our desire for closure, and in an age where the foreshadowing of sequels is not uncommon, we can accept this idea though it is not written in any of the play-texts we have for the play.

The same demand for closure is used to decide whether characters and events are believable. When Petruchio arrives late for his wedding with Katherine (in *The Taming of the Shrew*), we are not surprised because we have been shown his character. We expect him to do something unusual, even bizarre, and we are not disappointed by his lateness or by the strangeness of his costume when he arrives. Each translation must be read in the context of the time and place the film was made if we are to decide whether our reading is being 'fair' to the film. We cannot expect a film to be read against the historical, cultural and social context it was made in.

The demand for closure allows us to accept that the shrew, Katherine, may have come to love Petruchio but we expect her to maintain a strong individual identity. Shakespeare's play text supports a range of film interpretations which can all suit our demand for a realistic logic.

Director's Cut 1

In the opening scene of *Othello*, Iago is bitter because he has been passed over for Michael Cassio as Othello's lieutenant. He persuades Roderigo to reveal to Desdemona's father that Othello is making love with her. Because Roderigo is also in love with Desdemona, he is easily led into mischief intended to shame her and embarrass Othello. As a play, this opening introduces the major characters and establishes their relationships.

❖ Discuss the impact of the scene as the opening for a film.

❖ Othello is a strong general with a long battle record but he is black while Desdemona is white. Suggest possible openings for the play as film.

❖ Discuss the changes you would make if you were producing the film to: introduce elementary students to the excitement of Shakespeare; present a showcase of Canadian or Australian acting; take advantage of the multicultural nature of the audience; focus on the changing role of women in society.

Establishing Shot 3

The third element of narrative film-making is called **polarisation.** When opinions or objects are polarised, they are at opposite extremes of a possible range. Polarisation is the essential element for creating *dramatic conflict* in both literary and film narratives. Without conflict there is no need for *resolution* (solving the conflict or problem). Discuss the use of polarisation in Shakespearean text.

In most works of entertainment, reality is changed to create a narrative which fits within the time and budget available. By reducing subtle character differences and lengthy events, polarisation is used to cut time and costs while increasing dramatic effect.

The reasons for wars are simplified so that peace is polarised with violence; the extent and effect of crime is exaggerated so that crime is polarised with a need for detection and one police character represents all police so that justice becomes the clear opposite of injustice. In the real world, we know that these polarisations are often over-simplified, even unrealistic. We are all sometimes good, sometimes clever, sometimes successful. At other times we have 'a bad day'. In film, polarisation can be used to provide happy endings, justice and peace.

Most of us enjoy stories where things turn out happily in the end but happy endings depend on sad possibilities. Peaceful endings need violent events to stop. Like the cartoon character that runs through the wall or flies into the air in the explosion, we know that it is not reality we are watching but we *want* it to be like that.

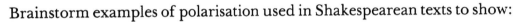

Cutaway 9
Take 1

Work in small groups to brainstorm the polarisations which are used in plays such as *Julius Caesar* and *King Lear* so that unhappy complications can be saved with happy resolutions.

Brainstorm examples of polarisation used in Shakespearean texts to show:

❖ Unhappy people who are made happy.

❖ Happy people who become unhappy.

Work in media watch teams to watch each of the different television news programs on a single evening. In your media watch group, decide who will make notes about each of the first, second, third, fourth news stories.

❖ For the story you are watching, list the goodies, the baddies and the event which makes the news. (Remember, polarisation can be between countries, groups, single people and even animals or natural events like earthquakes.)

❖ Use the information you have collected in your media watch team to make a chart which shows the polarisation in each news story.

❖ Discuss the way the news is constructed to simplify causes and solutions.

❖ Compare these with Shakespearean texts you have worked with.

❖ Write a short description of how polarisation works in one text you have worked with.

Working as a whole group, discuss whether the story is believable. Suggest how the camera angles and music can help the story.

Juliet finally persuades her nurse to let her meet with Romeo. Write the shooting script (camera directions and dialogue) from when Juliet knocks on the door until she is with Romeo.

Shakespearean audiences had to stand in the open during daylight to watch a play performed by actors using no special costume. The audience had to watch and listen carefully and they needed times to relax from tension. Shakespeare deliberately *polarised* his plays by *juxtaposing* comic sections in tragedies; common people in plays about kings and nobles. Most importantly, however, he included clear explanatory speeches which simplified issues by showing them as choices between clearly opposing options. Hamlet's famous soliloquy begins "To be or not to be, that is the question". He then presents his thoughts about the meaning of life as a life or death choice – to suffer life or to die (and risk eternal damnation – "what dreams may come ...").

Polarisation is so common that we often do not notice it. Most films are expected to be about two hours long and, on commercial television, they are interrupted with commercial breaks so that their length is probably about the same as in Elizabethan times. As a result, it can be argued, the development of plot and character we are familiar with has changed little, although both the technology and levels of audience comfort are very different.

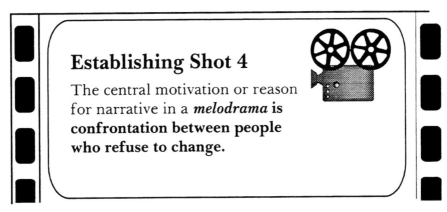

Establishing Shot 4

The central motivation or reason for narrative in a *melodrama* is **confrontation between people who refuse to change.**

In plays such as *Henry V* and *Richard III*, the central issues follow from a confrontation between individuals or groups who refuse to change what they believe to avoid or reduce conflict – the issue is polarised.

Key Shot

Tragedy: an event or sequence of events created because a character cannot moderate the intensity of a feeling or personal characteristic which could be desirable if not taken to the extreme.

When the refusal to change leads to disastrous results, the play is identified as a tragedy. Macbeth's ambition leads him to be greedy and ruthless. As a result, he destroys the peace of the kingdom he wants to rule over and is killed. King Lear is obsessed with being loved. His desire for love leads to the destruction of his family's happiness and his own death. *Shakespearean tragedies occur because the central character, the tragic hero, refuses to reduce the intensity of a usually worthy characteristic such as love or ambition.*

When the characteristic is less worthy of our deep consideration - such as the need for enjoyment or the need for speed - events resulting from a refusal to moderate behaviour usually create a *melodrama*.

Key Shot

Melodrama: the story is a confrontation between individuals or groups who refuse to change what they believe to avoid or reduce conflict.

Melodrama can seem very simple and childish when it is viewed from outside the event and some of Shakespeare's characters behave quite melodramatically - usually to create comedy. More often, the emotions they experience and the unlimited pursuit of these emotions leads them to generate events which must be seen more seriously. However, serious issues can be melodramatic and melodrama can result in tragic consequences. The similarity between the two elements can even be confusing. Love can produce comedy or tragedy. In *All's Well That Ends Well*, the jealousies could lead to tragedy if they were treated differently. In the comedies, Shakespeare's characters tend to learn from their mistakes and reach happy endings - or die. In tragedies, the inability to change, the tragic flaws in the heroes, leads them to their own destruction.

Cutaway 9
Take 2

We read about tragic accidents and tragic events in the newspapers and watch them on television. They always involve strong emotions.

❖ Discuss the difference between Shakespearean tragedy and media definitions of tragedy.

❖ Suggest how a car accident involving alcohol could be the basis of a Shakespearean tragedy. Who would become the tragic hero? Is this a useful way of exploring modern use of the term 'tragedy'?

In *Romeo and Juliet*, gang members are killed in the fighting between families but they are not tragic heroes.

❖ Discuss the difference between a tragic death and the death of a tragic hero.

Polarisation is important if we are going to believe that confrontation between characters or groups is possible. In a family argument, we need to know that different family members have different needs or beliefs before we can believe the argument will happen. In a war film, we need to know who is on each side and why they are fighting. The confrontation can be created by placing opposing forces next to each other and then bringing their stories together.

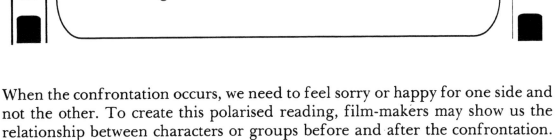

Establishing Shot 5

Juxtaposition is the process of placing unrelated shots or sequences next to each other. The effect can make us feel uncomfortable but it can also cause us to think about connecting information that we wouldn't have thought was connected.

When the confrontation occurs, we need to feel sorry or happy for one side and not the other. To create this polarised reading, film-makers may show us the relationship between characters or groups before and after the confrontation. The juxtaposition of people or events we like with people or events we do not like helps us to read the confrontation as the film-maker wants us to.

Cutaway 9
Take 3

Work as a media watch team to follow the juxtaposition of events in the second scene of Kenneth Branagh's film of *Henry V* – from his entry through the doors until he is given the tennis balls. Make a running sheet of the shots used and identify the juxtaposed shots.

Discuss the way the juxtaposition helps to identify the power relationships between characters to create a single reading of the events.

When Branagh's Henry V delivers his *Once more into the breach* speech, the fear of the soldiers is juxtaposed against the fury of the battle. Identify the juxtaposed shots and discuss the way they are used to create a feeling of action at the same time as they suggest Henry will be successful.

Films about war usually show pictures of the 'goodies' doing pleasing or happy things. Against this they juxtapose the 'baddies' looking unhappy and doing unpleasant things. How is juxtaposition used to create this feeling in the Agincourt battle scene from Branagh's *Henry V*. View the same scene from the Lawrence Olivier version of the film and discuss the differences. Make a running sheet of the shots used in the sequence from Olivier's film.

Label the juxtaposed shots and write a short description of the way juxtaposition can be used to create excitement in a film.

Chapter 10: Richard III

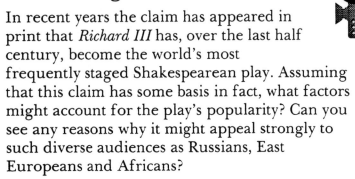

Establishing Shot 1

In recent years the claim has appeared in print that *Richard III* has, over the last half century, become the world's most frequently staged Shakespearean play. Assuming that this claim has some basis in fact, what factors might account for the play's popularity? Can you see any reasons why it might appeal strongly to such diverse audiences as Russians, East Europeans and Africans?

In the last half century, there have been four major attempts to transfer *Richard III* to the screen:

1955: Laurence Olivier's *Richard III* (London Film Productions).

1983: The BBC/Time-Life Television version. Director: Jane Howell.

1990: The English Shakespeare Company's *The Wars of the Roses: Richard III*. Director: Michael Bogdanov.

1996: Ian McKellen and Richard Loncraine's *Richard III* (United Artists).

In addition, there is Al Pacino's *Looking for Richard*, a semi-documentary act of homage to Shakespeare : "It has always been a dream of mine to communicate how I feel about Shakespeare to others." His film includes interviews with well known Shakespearean actors like Kenneth Branagh and Vanessa Redgrave, and looks at the casting for a production of *Richard III*. Then the film switches from actors discussing the text to early rehearsals and to scenes from the final, costumed version of the play. Incidentally, the claim that *Richard III* is Shakespeare's most frequently performed play is repeated here.

Clearly, one of the main aims of the film is to make *Richard III* accessible to the average filmgoer. The background of the Wars of the Roses is explained, and key scenes are performed. Several of these scenes are worth comparing with the same scenes in the other films. One has to admit, however, that the degree of self-indulgence exhibited in the film works against Pacino's aim; much of what we see should have ended on the cutting room floor.

This chapter concentrates on the Olivier and McKellen/Loncraine versions, both designed for the large screen. Some aspects of *Looking for Richard* are also considered, and the chapter ends with a note on the English Shakespeare Company's version, which forms the final part of an ambitious adaptation of the plays dealing with the Wars of the Roses.

Establishing Shot 2

Any director of play or film wishing to present Shakespeare today must decide on the period in which the play will be set. In Shakespeare's day, his history plays were performed in Elizabethan dress, on a largely bare stage, with the words alone signalling a past time. (It was only in the nineteenth century that directors began to strive for historical accuracy in dress.)

These days Shakespeare's plays are frequently presented in modern dress, but the motivation is very different – it is a deliberate shifting of the play to another time. Branagh's recent film of *Hamlet*, for example, has been given a mid-nineteenth century setting; a very successful Australian stage production of *As You Like It* was set in the Australian outback in the 1920s.

❖ What would cause a director to shift one of the history plays to another time?

Another stratagem sometimes adopted in Shakespearean productions is to use an eclectic variety of costuming in order to prevent the audience from placing the production in a specific historical time frame. What do you think of this idea? What is lost?

Historical Setting

Olivier chose to place his film in an obviously late medieval setting. The costuming is medieval fashion at its most elaborate: the women wear high conical hats with silk floating from the tops; the men have elaborate headgear and long pointed shoes.

Pacino, too, in the costumed scenes that we see, has opted for a medieval setting: filming takes place in The Cloisters, a medieval building transported stone by stone to New York and rebuilt as part of the Metropolitan Museum of Art's collection. Since Pacino is not trying to film the whole story, the scenes that he does include are uncut, and thus often closer to the original play-text than the corresponding scenes in the other two films.

In contrast, the McKellen/Loncraine film is set in the 1930s. The film is based on a highly successful Royal National Theatre production of the play, which was directed by Richard Eyre in 1990. McKellen has written:

> *The crucial advantage of a modern setting is clarity of storytelling. It is impossibly confusing to try and distinguish between a multitude of characters who are all done up in floppy hats and wrinkled tights.*
> (McKellen, 1996, p12)

It is clear, however, from his later comments, that he and Eyre selected the 1930s because they were "a decade of tyranny" – a time when "a dictatorship like Richard III's might have overtaken the United Kingdom, as it had done Germany, Italy, Spain and the empire of the Soviet Union" (p13). In other words, they were deliberately creating historical resonances.

Cutaway 10
Take 1

When reading the McKellen/Loncraine translation, watch for scenes which are structured to remind the audience of events from the 1930s.

After watching the Olivier film, consider McKellen's view that a medieval setting is "impossibly confusing" to a modern audience. Do you agree?

In small working groups, consider some other possible periods in which *Richard III* might be set. What difficulties can you see in trying to set the play in the future?

Establishing Shot 3

Even though it is based on historical events, *Richard III* is not a documentary. Shakespeare felt free to alter the facts as he knew them to suit his dramatic purpose; the directors of both film versions have exercised a similar freedom with Shakespeare's play-text. What are some of the factors that might weigh with the director when deciding on changes to the play-text?

Changes: from history to play-text; from play-text to film

As in his other history plays, Shakespeare compressed the action and made other alterations to the facts as he knew them. (It should be remembered that Shakespeare was drawing on Tudor sources, which had the essentially propagandist motive of justifying the Tudor Henry VII's seizure of the throne.)

He made the Lancastrian Prince Edward Anne's husband instead of simply her betrothed; he brought Queen Margaret to life (she had been dead at least a year when the action of the play begins); he had Richard slain by Richmond personally, rather than simply killed in the heat of battle.

Olivier's film translation makes a further group of changes, including the following:

- ❖ He begins with the final scene from the previous play in the sequence;
- ❖ Richard woos Anne over the corpse of her husband (in the play it is the corpse of her father-in-law, Henry VI);
- ❖ The discussion between the murderers of Clarence is cut;
- ❖ The role of Queen Margaret is cut;
- ❖ King Edward's mistress, Jane Shore, who does not appear in the play-text, appears wordlessly in several scenes in the film;
- ❖ Richmond's dream is omitted;
- ❖ Richard is slain by a group of soldiers, not by Richmond.

The McKellen/Loncraine translation, as well as shifting the story to the 1930s:

- ❖ removes Queen Margaret, giving some of her lines to the Duchess of York (played by Maggie Smith);
- ❖ drops the explanation of how Richard has managed to get Clarence imprisoned;
- ❖ brings Princess Elizabeth into the play;
- ❖ introduces Richmond much earlier;
- ❖ greatly shortens Richard's dream, and omits Richmond's dream;
- ❖ makes a large number of other changes, including some modernisation of the language (eg, removing the 'thous' and 'thees').

Director's Cut 1 – Opening Scenes

Shakespeare's play-text opens with Richard alone on stage. He reveals his plans – "I am determined to prove a villain" – and then sees the success of his first piece of plotting when Clarence enters under guard. Why might a film director feel that this is too stark an opening? What is a film audience likely to expect that the audience in Shakespeare's Globe Theatre would not? What is a modern audience likely to need that an Elizabethan audience would not?

Opening Scenes

After a foreword emphasising that many legends have accrued around England's crown (and hence that not all that follows should be taken as fact) Olivier's film begins with Act V, scene vii of *Henry VI, Part III*, which sees Edward IV crowned. As the courtiers shout "Long Live the King!", Gloucester exchanges a significant glance with Buckingham. We see the Queen with her children, and catch sight of Jane Shore, Edward's mistress. Later there is a royal progress through London's streets, leaving Richard alone in the coronation hall. He delivers the play's opening soliloquy, with interpolated lines stressing the number of lives that lie between him and the throne. The British film critic, Roger Manvell, observed that:

The total speech, played in a single six-minute take in the large, empty L-shaped set of the coronation hall, is spoken direct to the camera, some parts of it intimately, ironically, in close-shot, other parts, especially those which are almost paranoically loud-mouthed, spoken from a distance, the camera following Gloucester into the other wing of the hall where the King's throne is set, surmounted by a vast, pendant crown. Gloucester asks for our appreciation with his slyly upturned eyes, his knowing nods and glances, and the humorous delight he takes in his own astute villainy. But behind these attractive touches lies the sinister obsession of his megalomania, and the devilish pacing of his crow-like feet, shod in black shoes with long, pointed toes. (Manvell, 1971, p49)

McKellen's opening scenes step back even further into *Henry VI, Part III*. The Battle of Tewkesbury is in progress, with news coming in by tickertape to Lancastrian headquarters, a country house. Prince Edward of Lancaster, having said goodnight to his father, sits at his desk, on which is a photograph of his wife, Lady Anne. He is startled by a rumbling noise. Then a tank crashes through the wall, the Prince and his guards are shot. One of the figures in a gas mask is revealed as Richard of Gloucester, who goes on to shoot King Henry VI. McKellen writes: "It is appropriate that Richard's face should at first sight be masked – as are his feelings from the world." (McKellen, 1996, p46)

There is a swift transition to the Palace, where King Edward IV, his Queen and their children are establishing themselves. We see King Edward getting ready for the Victory Ball, but his ill health is suggested by his having to take some medicine. The difference between the murderously active Richard and his brother Clarence is suggested by showing Clarence as an enthusiastic amateur photographer (a passive recorder of events rather than an active participant). Another scene change shows the Queen's brother, Earl Rivers, arriving by plane

---

Cutaway 10
Take 2

In Olivier's film translation of *Hamlet*, the soliloquies are delivered mainly by voice-over, as though unspoken thoughts. In the two film translations, we are considering scenes where the actors have taken the decision to direct their soliloquies to the camera.

Briefly research what Shakespearean scholars currently believe were the uses of soliloquy in the Elizabethan theatre.

❖ Was the actor talking directly to the audience, or was he talking to himself?

❖ Which do you consider to be the better way of dealing with the problem of Shakespeare's soliloquies?

❖ Considering their characters, their likely ages and their motivations, discuss whether you, as a filmmaker or film director, would choose the same method for Hamlet's soliloquies as for Richard's.

❖ In what ways does Pacino's delivery of Richard's first soliloquy differ from Olivier's?

---

from America. (In the play, Richard detests the Woodvilles, the Queen and her brothers, as social upstarts who are making the most of their new-won power; a 1930s equivalent was to make them Americans, echoing the liaison between another Edward and Mrs Simpson.)

The Victory Ball swings into action, with a singer, backed by a dance band, singing a catchy tune with words by Christopher Marlowe. (Note the initials on the band's music stands.) The scene will remind many experienced viewers of Dennis Potter's tv series *The Singing Detective*). Richard's opening words in the play become a victory toast to the King, but the second part of the speech is delivered in the men's washroom, where Richard can look at himself in the mirror. Like Olivier, McKellen has chosen to direct his soliloquy to the camera.

But note the contrast between Olivier's six-minute take and the swift juxtaposition of scenes in the McKellen film.

Cutaway 10
Take 3

In your group, look carefully at McKellen/Loncraine's handling of the ballroom scene. A great deal of information is conveyed about the characters and their relationship to one another, information that it would be impossible for a stage audience to pick up, apart from those sitting in the front rows. The scene cleverly helps the audience to sort out all the characters, but in addition it conveys the tensions and anxieties of the court. What do we pick up about the relationship between Richard and Buckingham? What indications are given of the court's attitude to the Queen and her brother? What is conveyed of Richard's relationship with his mother?

Director's Cut 2 – The Wooing Scene(s)

In one of the most startling scenes in Shakespeare, and one of the most difficult to make at all credible, Shakespeare's Richard woos and wins Anne in the space of a single scene (I.ii.33-225).

❖ How would you, as a director, make Anne's yielding to Richard convincing?

Olivier's solution is to split the wooing into two scenes, thus suggesting a time lapse. The corpse is not that of Henry VI but of Prince Edward of Lancaster, Anne's husband. Anne, played by Claire Bloom, seems to succumb to Richard's sexual magnetism. McKellen has the scene played in its original form, but, like Olivier, makes the corpse that of Anne's husband. A careful comparison of the two versions is worthwhile. Does the splitting of the scene into two aid credibility? Does the background of the mortuary in McKellen's version strengthen the impact of the scene?

The wooing scene is also included in *Looking for Richard.* Here the corpse is that of Henry VI, as in the original play, and here Anne capitulates completely. How do you think it compares with the same scene(s) in the two films of *Richard III*?

Director's Cut 3 – Point of View

It is argued that the film director can control the audience's point of view and limit the range of audience response more effectively than a stage director can with a play.

In Olivier's film, watch for:

❖ the number of times the camera focuses on the crown;

❖ the use of close-ups, particularly of Richard.

Carefully view the close-ups of Richard in the McKellen/Loncraine film, especially after one of his victims dies, and also after his encounters with his mother. McKellen (1996, p23) states that he is seeking to show Richard's 'inner moral turmoil'. Does he succeed?

In your group, discuss the view of Richard that each film seems to wish us to take. Which Richard seems the more evil? Does either Richard seem the embodiment of pure evil? If not, what redeeming qualities does either of them have?

McKellen's film gives much more space to the Queen, her children, and her brother. How does this affect our view of Richard?

And what of Pacino's translation? What differences do you notice between his Richard and Olivier's?

Director's Cut 4 – Polarisation

In planning their film of *Richard III,* McKellen and Loncraine clearly felt the need to create a stronger counterbalance to Richard than is provided in Shakespeare's play-text. Hence the prominence they have provided for Queen Elizabeth, giving her scenes that are not in the original play, and many lines that in Shakespeare's play-text belong to other characters. In your group, compare the roles given to Queen Elizabeth in the two films and analyse their effect. Does Olivier's film lose in impact by not having a strong counterbalance for

Visual Effects

Note, in Olivier's film:

❖ the repeated image of the crown;

❖ the constant use of Richard's shadow to sinister effect throughout (and contrasting with Richard's reactions to his dream – "...shadows tonight/Have struck more terror to the soul of Richard/Than can the substance of ten thousand soldiers...")

- the effect of flaming torches coming in from all angles in the scene in the palace when Richard receives messengers who all bear bad news;

- at the Battle of Bosworth Field, the image of the crown rolling in the dust of the battlefield.

Cutaway 10
Take 4

What visual touches would you select as particularly effective in the McKellen/Loncraine film?

Director's Cut 5 – Intertextuality

All texts reflect back to other texts, a feature known as **intertextuality**. Sometimes this is very obvious, as in the large number of films that remind us of the story of Cinderella. But such intertextuality is not only to be found in the storyline: in Branagh's film of *Much Ado About Nothing*, for example, the opening scene is a deliberate reminder of an earlier film, *The Magnificent Seven.*

- Are there any other ways in which intertextuality, deliberate or otherwise, can occur in films?

- What examples of intertextuality can you find in either of the translations of *Richard III?*

Film Music

In both films, music plays an important part. Sir William Walton's music was, Olivier thought, "a lifesaver" in helping overcome the film's weakest part, the battle sequence (Olivier, 1982, pp162-3), though some thought it too melodramatic at the point of Richard's death. Loncraine's choice of jazz and swing at significant points, such as the song at the Victory Ball, creates a totally different emotional response.

Cutaway 10
Take 5

Compare the musical choices made to support our viewing response to Richard's choice of record as he contemplates the photos of Hastings' execution.

- Discuss the effectiveness of each musical choice in terms of the way it supports the translation of the scene.

A Note on *The Wars of the Roses*

This is a film version, difficult to acquire, of Michael Bogdanov's epic condensation of the three parts of *Henry VI* and *Richard III*. (The English Shakespeare Company took the play on a tour of Australia and North America after its success in Britain.) The film is certainly worth seeing, but its particular significance from our point of view is that, like the later McKellen/Loncraine film, *The Wars of the Roses* has a setting that begins in the 1930s. It ends in the present day, with Richmond's victory speech a televised press conference, but at the Battle of Bosworth, the smoke clears and Richard and Richmond are seen fighting their final duel dressed in armour, one in gold, the other in black, and wielding broadswords.

Further Opportunities for Discussion

1. When Olivier's film was released, it was generally praised, though most critics have found it inferior to his *Henry V* and his later *Hamlet*. The McKellen/Loncraine film, on the other hand, has sharply divided the critics. Here are two contrasting views:

    McKellen's performance is far more successful on film than it was on stage, in part because the proximity of the camera breaks through the surface armour of his icy characterisation. As in the stage production, McKellen eschews the traditional majesty and charisma associated with Olivier, who flaunted sexual magnetism and athletic vigour in spite of his limp and hump. Though McKellen gives asides and soliloquies directly to the camera, as Olivier did, he rarely ingratiates himself; he is no charming Vice-figure but a haggard, sleepless killer...[I]n the film his work comes across as more nuanced and complex. The camera catches his relationships to the other characters in subtle details: the amused affection with which he offers chocolates to Tyrell, the glinting malice with which he flatters Hastings just before condemning him... (Loehlin, 1997, p75)

    and

    ... a parody of Hollywood films, at times mildly amusing, most of the time simply grotesque - a shallow, meretricious shadow of the stage production. ... As with other anachronistic productions of a script ... we have two plays competing against each other, with the Shakespeare script a distant runner-up. (Coursen, 1997, pp141,143)

    What do *you* think?

2. Both Olivier and McKellen deliver their soliloquies and asides directly to the camera, and thus to us, the viewers. Do you detect any differences in the way they do this, and in the effect it has on us?

3 . A scene that is included in all three films is the council scene called to consider the young prince's coronation. (Pacino's film gives the scene without cuts.) A comparison of all three scenes will allow you not only to look at the different interpretations, but also at the directors' use of close ups to convey the changing feelings of the participants more subtly than is possible on stage. Which of the three do you consider the most successful?

4. Do you think Pacino has succeeded in his attempt to make Shakespeare accessible to the average filmgoer?

For a parodied version of *Richard III*,
see Neil Simon's film, *The Goodbye Girl.*

Chapter 11: King Lear

Establishing Shot

Although scholars and critics view *King Lear* as a complex and rewarding play, many audiences have described the play as "dark, treacherous and painful". Directors, too, have different visions of the play, ranging from Peter Brook's 1969 "bleak and existential" television version, dubbed "the night of the living dead" by Pauline Kael, to Michael Elliott's 1984 version, described as a "symphonic poem," which focuses on Lear's sufering and the understandings and changes in attitude that Lear arrives at through this suffering. (Rothwell and Melzer, p135). On a more positive note, O'Brien (1982) describes Lear as "... everyman with a common history":

Sympathy with Lear is sympathy with the particularity of human suffering, human folly, human need, human bewilderment. Lear gains as much wisdom as a man can gain, without losing a jot of his individuality...His simplest utterances open a shaft to the depths of experience. (O'Brien, 1982: 76).

Cutaway 11
Take 1

As you view multiple versions of *King Lear*, judge which directors and leading actors have the best sense of this sympathy with human suffering which O'Brien sees as central to the play.

The discussion in this chapter explores three film versions of *King Lear*: the Peter Brook and Michael Elliott versions noted above, and an earlier version by Brook (1953) which stars Orson Welles (who has also played in film translations of *Macbeth* and *Othello*).

Key Shot – Production Data

Production data on these three versions, along with notes on a variety of other productions (including spoofs and parodies), are found toward the end of the chapter.

Directors

While films are frequently known by their stars – the 'Lawrence Olivier *Hamlet*', the 'Marlon Brando *Julius Caesar*' or the 'Mel Gibson *Hamlet*' – it is the director's vision that provides the foundation for the translation of the play-text to film.

Between the director's or producer's initial idea for a film and the opening week in the cinema, years may pass. Because of lengthy production schedules and because any individual movie provides a director with the opportunity to present only a part of his or her world vision (or *Weltanschauung*), directors seldom produce two different versions of the same play or film script.

King Lear, however, is an exception. Two of the three major film versions of *King Lear* were directed by Peter Brook. The 1953 version, co-directed by Andrew McCullough, was made for television viewing and starred Orson Welles (who shortly afterwards directed his own version of *Macbeth*). The 1969 film version starred Paul Schofield.

Brook's twin interpretations provide a rare opportunity to examine how the director's vision of the play has changed over the years, how the film techniques he uses have developed and grown and, incidentally, how television filming for a small screen is necessarily different from cinematic filming for a large screen.

In this chapter we explore Peter Brook's changing conception of the overall effect of the play (if this were the same for both versions, there would be no need for the second version); his differing use of settings, costumes, sound and music; the impact of casting on interpretation; and his use of techniques such as camera angles and close ups.

Director's Cut 1

The social context of Britain changed substantially between the two translations. Recovery from damage caused by extensive bombing during the Second World War and an even slower economic recovery left many feeling that their lives were irrecoverably changed. By 1969, post-war recovery had taken place and a new generation was demanding an end to Britain's nuclear involvement, an improved sharing of wealth and a new social order. In this context, consider the choices the director has made: black and white or colour? the use of horse-drawn carriages? *King Lear* set mid-winter? In addition, it is worth looking at the various ways the director tampered with Shakespeare's play-text. Are the director's cuts similar in the two versions? Are scenes or parts of scenes presented in a different order?

At the same time, the third major film version – directed by Michael Elliott and starring Sir Lawrence Olivier – provides contrasts in both technique and vision.

The Divine Right of Kings

Before exploring the three film productions in detail, it is worth noting the exalted position of the King. In each of the three film versions, the King's absolute authority over all matters within the kingdom is evident. However, each of the three films uses a different way of demonstrating the power that the king exerts over his subjects.

Cutaway 11
Take 2

Working in small groups, research the changing meaning of the term 'The Divine Right of Kings'. Discuss how this right might have affected the way Shakespeare's audiences would have viewed the absolute power that Kings and Queens had over their subjects. Compare the degrees of this belief which appear to underlie the three film versions of *Lear*.

In modern democracies, when leaders retire, others rise immediately and apparently naturally to take their places. However, in Lear's time – and indeed to a lesser extent in Shakespeare's time – the monarch held absolute power and the fortunes of the country depended almost entirely on the decisions made by him or her. The orderly succession of power from one ruler to the next, then, was of life-and-death concern to all of the subjects. The savage unrest and uncertainty caused by the replacement of the Catholic Queen Mary with the Protestant Queen Elizabeth is clearly portrayed in the recent film *Elizabeth* (1998) and the legalisation of divorce by Henry VIII would be very clear in the minds of the Shakespearean audience.

Cutaway 11
Take 3

In 1601, the Earl of Essex led a revolt against Queen Elizabeth. He was arrested and beheaded. In 1603, Elizabeth died and James VI of Scotland became James I of England. Sir Walter Raleigh, a former favourite of Elizabeth, was beheaded shortly afterwards. By the end of 1605, Guy Fawkes had been executed for leading a conspiracy against the English parliament. *King Lear* was first performed at some point during this time. Suggest why it was important for Shakespeare's theatre company that the Duke of Albany should return the throne to its rightful successor before the close of the play.

At a point in western history when the President of the United States can be impeached for lying about his personal behaviour at the same time as he is directing one of the most advanced armed forces in the world, it is important that, as modern audiences, we are reminded of the absolute authority of the monarch from whose edicts there is no appeal. We need to recall the Queen of Hearts in Lewis Carroll's *Alice in Wonderland* whose favourite line when anyone displeased her was "Off with his head". Two of Henry VIII's wives were beheaded for displeasing their husband.

Cutaway 11
Take 4

Research the origins of Lewis Carroll's Queen of Hearts from *Alice in Wonderland*. Is she modelled on a real Queen? Are there any Kings or Queens in British history who would provide appropriate models for Carroll's Queen of Hearts?

Which of Henry VIII's wives were beheaded? What was their crime? Did it affect inheritance? Who were the next four successors to Henry VIII as ruler and what was the relationship of each to Henry VIII?

Explore the relationship between the plot of *King Lear* and the resulting succession of Queens following the death of Henry VIII.

Two obvious examples of the King's power found in the Lear script are the banishment of Kent and Lear's authority to divide up the kingdom without apparently consulting with anyone. Since he *owns* the country, he can divide it in any way he sees fit.

While each director works with the same basic facts, the visual medium of the film affords many opportunities to either emphasise or minimise the absolute power of the ruler. We note below several ways that each director emphasises the King's authority – for example, in the 1969 Brook/Schofield production, those who the King authorises to speak are passed the Orb – but you should be on the lookout for other subtle indicators as you view the various versions (eg, what is the effect of Kent being commanded to kneel in the Brook/Schofield version?).

Openings

Most of the revealing comparisons and contrasts in the three film versions of *King Lear* can be gathered from a careful examination of the first act.

Indeed, if you were preparing for a test and didn't have time to reread an entire play or novel, it could be useful to review the first act or chapter: what will happen in the remainder of the play or novel is almost always set up in the opening scenes and lines.

Below we examine the opening of the play through exploring the cinematic techniques used to present Lear's character

Initial Impressions of King Lear

Initial impressions of characters in films and plays – much as initial impressions of people in life – come from their physical appearance, their attire, their speech (both what they say and how they say it), and other people's reactions to them.

In all three major film versions, when we first meet the King, he is bearded and speaks with authority. People listen carefully to him; all attention is on him. However, each film presents a somewhat different Lear, too.

Camera Work

In the Brook/Schofield translation, what is the effect of the close-up of Lear's face, lighted from the front and top, surrounded by darkness?

What is the effect of the mid-shot in the Brook/Welles translation?

Comment on the camera angles which precede the appearance of Lear in each translation: what is the effect of panning across the unemotional faces of people in the Brook/Welles translation? In this scene, the camera moves first in one direction and then in another. Contrast the subjects' expressions in the two different camera movements.

In the Brook/Welles translation, the camera enters the throne room from behind, revealing a huge slab of rock which turns out to be the back of the throne; in the background, people are seated.. What is the effect of this image? As is noted below, the Elliott/Olivier translation illustrates the respect commanded by Lear in a very striking image of nobility paying homage to Lear.

Reactions of Other Characters

In the Elliott/Olivier translation, true to Shakespeare's play-text, we are introduced to the King by two nobles and the illegitimate son of one of them. They are making small talk while waiting for the King to arrive. It is clear from their conversation that, not unlike modern government press conferences, the King's impending announcement is an *open secret*.

What is the effect, then, in the following scene when these nobles and every other noble in the room, including the King's daughters, lie prostrate – flat on their stomachs, faces on the ground – with their arms outstretched toward the King as he mounts the throne?

It is interesting to speculate on how Shakespeare's theatre company would have shown Lear's absolute power on the stage of the Globe Theatre (or would there be any need to do so since all theatre goers would be intimately acquainted with the absolute powers of the monarch and the need to show obedience in various ways?).

Cutaway 11
Take 5

Research histories of England to explore whether prostration as a method of showing obeisance was used in England. Or was it imported from Asia during the twentieth century, finding its way into our ideas about how submissiveness is shown? It is useful to view the first entrance of Branagh's *Henry V* into his court for a comparison of ways in which the camera can be used as a character to create a sense of the King's power.

In other translations, the trappings of majesty are also evident. In the Brook/Welles version, it is assumed that the King has the right to speak. Before any other characters – including the King's daughters – can speak, however, they must be granted the authority to do so by being passed the Orb which they hold in front of them.

Key Shot – Symbolism

It is interesting that Peter Brook chose the Orb as the symbol of authority because an Orb is generally carried by a sovereign at a coronation. His interpretation suggests that whoever carried the orb had the authority of the King. The symbol of the Speaker's authority in Westminster parliamentary systems (Britain, Canada, Australia, New Zealand and some other British Commonwealth countries) is the mace. The ceremonial mace has its origins in the sceptre which has its roots in the shepherd's crook.

Many cultures have formal speaking rituals which require a speaker to hold some object whilst speaking to the group. The Kwagiulth Aboriginal people (also corrupted to Kwakiutl) of British Columbia and the Maoris of New Zealand, for example, both used 'talking sticks', canelike objects which speakers held whilst speaking to formal gatherings.

Note Lear's response when Kent violates this rule of the speaker and blurts out his challenge to Lear's division of the kingdom.

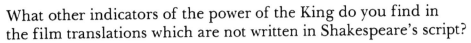

> ## Cutaway 11
> ## Take 6
>
> What other indicators of the power of the King do you find in the film translations which are not written in Shakespeare's script?
>
> Research the ongoing symbolism of 'maces,' 'orbs,' 'sceptres,' and 'talking sticks'. Present your research findings as a poster including pictorial and written findings.

The hall scene at Albany's Palace (Act I,iv) provides insights into the directors' views of Lear's character. As we watch Welles (Brook's first Lear) interact with his men, we observe the relationship he has with them. This contrasts sharply with the character of the Lears in other film versions. It is useful to discuss the physical distance between Lear and his men, the differences in the way that the knights and squires speak to each Lear, Lear's warmth toward his knights and squires, and even the physical proximity with the Fool.

> ## Cutaway 11
> ## Take 7
>
> Do the costumes worn by Lear in the different productions make a difference to the way we view his character?
>
> Which Lear seems to have been most successful at carrying out Lear's purpose 'To shake all cares and business of our age/Conferring them on younger strengths while we/ Unburthen'd crawl toward death'? (I,i,40-43).
>
> What is the effect of having Lear race his horse across the winter landscape in the Brook/Schofield version?
>
> If you have access to other film versions of *King Lear*, use the criteria above to contrast the image of Lear in the initial throne room scene with Lear in the hall at Albany's Palace.

Lear's Voice

In each of the three translations above, Lear is played by a world-famous actor well advanced in his career. Therefore, we can assume that each actor (in consultation with his director) has given considerable thought to how he will use his voice to build an initial impression of Lear. Close your eyes and listen to the voice of King Lear at the opening of each version.

Notice how each actor strikes the tricky balance between the Lear who appears to have grown weary of managing the kingdom (the occasion in the first scene is, after all, the announcement of the absolute monarch's impending retirement to the good life of hunting and male bonding) and the Lear whose voice was the difference between life and death, between the security of belonging to the commonwealth and the perils of banishment?

**Cutaway 11
Take 8**

Develop a set of criteria on which to judge voice (eg, rate of delivery, volume of voice, strength of voice, use of pauses, deliberateness, timbre, and resonance) and apply these to as many film versions of *Lear* as you can.

The Supporting Cast

To establish a credible translation of the Shakespearean play-text, the supporting actors need to be established economically and early, capturing the audience's attention, presenting their credentials, creating acting space for themselves. In *King Lear*, four characters are usually singled out for attention – Regan, Goneril, Cordelia, and Albany.

In any complex translation of King Lear, the roles of apparently lesser characters such as the Fool, Edgar, Kent, Edmund, and Cornwall can be used to strengthen or weaken the effect of more substantial characters. The role of the fool in Elizabethan theatre is particularly critical (for further detail see the note on the Fool in the chapter on *Twelfth Night*). Keep in mind, of course, that plays and films can be enhanced or marred by the performances of even relatively minor supporting characters (consider Jack Lemmon in Branagh's *Hamlet*).

Goneril is the first sister asked to profess her love for her father, but each of the three actresses playing Goneril (Beatrice Straight in Brook/Welles; Irene Worth in Brook/Schofield, and Dorothy Tutin in Elliott/Olivier) presents a somewhat different princess. All three have very similar lines to deliver, but their appearances (the way each wears her hair; costumes; jewellery), demeanours (postures, movements, facial expressions), and voices (tone, pitch, rate of presentation) demonstrate different interpretations of the character.

**Cutaway 11
Take 9**

Working in small viewing groups and using the criteria suggested above, together with criteria you develop yourself, identify and describe the effect of contrasts among the three interpretations of Goneril. Discuss the appropriateness of the character introduced as Goneril in each of the three versions with the Goneril who must farewell Cordelia later in the scene and then engage in a tête-à-tête with Regan shortly thereafter. Which of the actresses best foreshadows the callous Goneril we meet in the hall scene at Albany's Palace?

Some film versions include Cordelia's aside to the audience regarding Goneril's profession of love for Lear. Other versions omit this. What effect does the omission have on our initial impressions of Goneril?

Sexuality in Lear

Under Elliott's direction, Goneril and Regan each shows tendencies toward inappropriate sexual behavior early in the film. Goneril, for example, at the beginning of the hall scene in Albany's Palace, appears to be flirting with her servant Oswald. The inappropriate sexual behavior of Goneril and Regan begins later in the play in both of Brook's translations.

Cutaway 11
Take 10

Describe your responses to Goneril's actions in the hall scene at Albany's palace and compare them with those provoked by the same scene in each of the Peter Brook translations. Discuss the importance of this scene as a preparation for Goneril's betrayal of her husband in the final act. Is there any evidence in Shakespeare's script to support this?

Regan, as the middle child of three in her family, would probably have needed to work hard to set herself apart from her sisters. In all three translations of *Lear*, Regan is introduced as the middle child, the one who is left to repeat her older sister's praises, adding what she can, one not in line for the 'more opulent third' to be given her younger sister. It is, however, worth contrasting Diana Rigg's Regan (Elliott/Olivier) with those of the two Brook translations (Margaret Phillips in Brook/Welles, Susan Engel in Brook/Schofield).

Cutaway 11
Take 11

What words might be used to characterise the relationship between Lear and Regan in the Elliott/Olivier translation as Lear motions to her to demonstrate her subservience? What do you notice about Lear's and Regan's facial expressions? While Shakespeare's script does not suggest this, Elliott clearly felt that it contributed to the film. Is it an innocent, light hearted game between father and daughter, or is there something more sinister being implied here?

Possibly the most rewarding contrasts between the translations are the initial images of **Cordelia** in the Brook/Schofield translation because her asides are omitted from the opening scene. As a result, we are deprived of her initial thoughts and forced to evaluate our reaction to her on the basis of her appearance and those cutaway shots which allow us to see how she sees others at court and how they see her.

**Cutaway 11
Take 12**

Contrast the initial throneroom scene in this translation with at least one other translation to examine the initial believability of Cordelia.

Which Cordelia seems more genuine?

What is gained by omitting Cordelia's asides? Contrast the Brook/Schofield Cordelia (Anne-lise Gabold) with the Brook/Welles Cordelia (Natasha Parry) and/or the Elliott/Olivier Cordelia (Anna Calder-Marshall), and with the respective Gonerils and Regans.

Which Cordelia has more regal bearing?

Which Cordelia appears to have the qualities needed to become Queen of France?

Which Cordelia, in your opinion, is most likely to be able to lead the French troops in battle later in the play?

The Duke of Albany does not seem to be a role that stars would line up to try out for. However, the part is not an easy one: Albany has the task of standing in the wings at the opening of the play as his wife Goneril shares the spotlight with Lear. He becomes a person of no consequence in the hall scene where Goneril offends Lear.

In the second half of the play he must change from the 'cowish' (IV,ii,12), 'milk-livered man' (IV, ii, 50) described by Goneril to the decisive regent in the final act. With a minimum of lines to develop his role from, he must establish the character who gives commands, restores order and, ultimately, sets the ship of state back on course.

**Cutaway 11
Take 13**

What does Albany, the 'wallflower' in the first half of the play, do to prepare us for the regent who emerges in the final scenes of the play?

The three actors cast to play the difficult role of Albany (Arnold Moss in Brook/Welles; Cyril Cusack in Brook/Schofield; and Robert Lang in Elliott/Olivier) each presents a different persona for Albany in the first half of the play.

**Cutaway 11
Take 14**

Using two or more of the available film translations, compare the presentation of Albany (bearing, attire, voice, strength of his language, reactions of other characters to him) in the throne room scene (I,i) and the palace hall scene (I,iv).

Which Albany seems to be a more believable future leader of an army and king of the country.

Early in Act IV (Scene ii), Shakespeare's Albany becomes forceful in his berating of his wife: 'O Goneril, You are not worth the dust which the rude wind/Blows in your face' (35-37), 'Wisdom and goodness to the vile seem vile' (38) and 'See thyself, devil!' (59).

As O'Brien (1982) points out, in this scene Albany recognises and rejects evil, a stark contrast to the vulgarity of Goneril and Regan. Which actor, in your opinion, makes the most convincing conversion from wimp to master?

Supporting Actors

It is worth making similar comparisons of the actors who play the Fool and the Duke of Cornwall. Rosenberg characterised Alan Badel's performance as the Fool (Brook/Welles) as 'a restless acrobat who tried ineffectively to talk as he bounced' (Rothwell and Melzer, p132).

Cutaway 11
Take 15

Contrast Badel's performance with that of Jack MacGowran (Brook/Schofield) and John Hurt (Elliott/Olivier).

Which Fool is most likely to keep the King's favour whilst poking fun at the King's follies?

Which Fool seems most likely to be out of reach when the King's whip falls?

Performances

While the goodness of Cordelia and Kent or the evil of Goneril and Regan might limit the latitude of the performers in these roles, the complexities of the role of Lear invite a variety of performances and interpretations.

It has been argued that there is a certain playfulness and humanity in Olivier's performance which is lacking in those of Welles and Schofield. Collecting evidence to discuss this argument requires a careful examination of Olivier's entrance: what atmosphere is created by his holding onto Cordelia and apparently joking with her as he enters the throne room? As serious film readers, we might also focus on his kidding with Regan as she prepares to tell him how much she loves him and contrast this with his stern demand – only moments earlier – that Goneril kiss the rug. Olivier's facial expression in this scene is particularly noteworthy as we consider the effect of using the camera to focus on an apparent twinkle in his eye, and observe the playfulness (or is it mean teasing?) when he appears to invite Regan to kiss his ring. If these initial glimpses of Olivier's Lear are described as playful and warm, what words could be used to describe the initial Lear of Welles or Schofield?

Parody and Lear

Successful comedians often get laughs by mimicking famous people. Rich Little, for example, made a career of mimicking the voices of famous politicians, putting words in their mouths that had a ring of truth and, for the most part, a good deal of exaggeration. List mimics you know and identify the people they mimicked.

Of course, mimics do not often try to imitate everything that the person does. More often, they choose one or two characteristics – a twang, a drawl, the pitch of the voice, the rate of delivery of speech – but they do enough to create a recognizable *persona*.

Film Versions

Rothwell and Melzer (1990) list 44 versions and adaptations of *King Lear* which fall into four general categories:

- Full length movie productions with sets;
- Films or videotapes of stage versions;
- Educational productions – generally short films designed to explore a particular scene or theme – whose purpose is to instruct rather than to entertain; and
- Adaptations, derivatives, spoofs, or productions exploring parallel themes.

Four full length productions and four adaptations/parodies are described below.

1. Major productions

Four versions of *King Lear* produced over the forty-five years take different production slants and offer interesting opportunities for comparison:

- *King Lear* (1953). Because it was co-directed by Peter Brook who also directed a full length production in (1969) and because it stars Orson Welles, this short (73 minute) film elicits more interest than it otherwise would. The major shortcoming of this version is that it cuts entirely the subplot of the evil illegitimate son Edmund, the part of the play Shakespeare adapted from Sidney's *Arcadia*. As noted above, this causes several problems with the audience's preparation for the final fight between Edgar and Edmund.

- *King Lear* (1969). Director: Peter Brook; Lear: Paul Schofield. In Brook's words, he presented 'Shakespeare's rough, uneven, jagged, and disconcerting vision' (Rothwell and Melzer, p135). Schofield's Lear is frequently cited as 'one more sinning than sinn'd against,' citing Proudfoot's response. Although Shakespearean scholar Frank Kermode felt that this production was very good and underrated, a more common view was that of Pauline Kael: "Peter Brook's King Lear is grey and cold, and the actors have dead eyes. I didn't just dislike this production; I hated it...The conception is resolutely joyless and unbeautiful – a 'Lear' without passion, 'Lear' set in a glacial desert." (Rothwell and Melzer, p135).

- *King Lear* (1982). Director: Jonathan Miller; Lear: Michael Horden. From the BBC series 'The Shakespeare Plays,' this film was designed for television viewers. Horden won critical acclaim for his performance, his interpretation of Lear being a bumbler rather than a tyrant.

- *King Lear* (1984). Director: Michael Elliot; Lear: Sir Lawrence Olivier. This production was generally well received and critics praised it both for its vision of Lear (focusing on his suffering and his conversion) and for its overall effect: Rothwell and Melzer describe this version as a 'symphonic poem' similar to Franz Liszt's *Dante*.

2. Adaptations, derivatives and parodies

When directors choose the screen rather than the stage as the medium for Shakespearean plays, the productions are still quite obviously Shakespearean: the plot, the language, the script are all very similar to those watched by Shakespeare's audiences.

However, when film-makers are intrigued with the themes of the plays rather than the scripts, seeing the connection between the adaptation and the original play is not always easy.

Each of the four films outlined below was made for general audiences, so the debt to Shakespeare may or may not be obvious.

❖ *Broken Lance* (1954). Although *Broken Lance* is frequently cited as a derivative of *King Lear*, the connection is somewhat tenuous. The protagonist of the movie, Mat Devereux, has four sons, three of whom are disloyal (similar inclinations to those of the children of both Lear and Gloucester). Like Lear, Devereux is out of touch with the times. Both Spencer Tracy (Devereux) and E. G. Marshall were stars at the time the film was made, but three of Tracy's stage sons – Robert Wagner, Richard Widmark, and Hugh O'Brian – went on to become stars in their own rights.

❖ *The Dresser* (1985). On one level, this is a play about the relationship between a star and his valet, but on other levels, it is indebted to Shakespeare. First, Albert Finney, the star of a troupe of travelling Shakespearean actors in Great Britain, performs scenes from *King Lear* as an actor, a central part of the movie. However, the backstage look at the troupe suggests parallels with Lear: 'Sir,' the over-the-hill Shakespearean actor is a real-life 'Lear' while his 'Dresser' Norman plays the part of the fool.

❖ *Ran* (English translation: *Chaos*). (1985). In this Japanese adaptation of *King Lear*, three sons of a medieval Japanese warlord, Hidetora, feud over the power that their ageing father can no longer exercise. Hidetora bestows his authority but not his royal titles on his eldest son, Taro, but his other two sons object and the youngest is banished for his insolence. However the evil in the movie is vested in Taro's wife, Lady Kaede, not the children, Goneril and Regan. A documentary *The Making of Ran* is also available (see Rothwell and Melzer, p. 144). Although it can be found on public television from time to time, *Ran* is not generally recommended for viewing in secondary schools; however, students may find it extremely interesting to identify the cultural differences which are responsible for the adaptations in the Japanese version.

❖ *Lear* (1987). In this derivative/spoof of *King Lear*, Pulitzer Prize winning author Norman Mailer revises the play as an allegory for the struggle for power in the modern-day Mafia. Added to the mix is Shakespeare's great-great-great (thirteen times) grandson who feels destined to film a late-twentieth century production of *King Lear*. The all-star cast (Peter Sellars, Burgess Meredith, Molly Ringwald, and Woody Allen) might predict a strong production, but the critics either panned or ignored it and it is now usually seen only on late night television.

Further Opportunities for Discussion

List characters in any of the three major film translations of *King Lear* who have distinctive voices. Trace the characters through the films and note specific examples of times their voices help you to keep the characters distinct.

Section 5
Closure

Chapter 12
But What
Happened in the End?

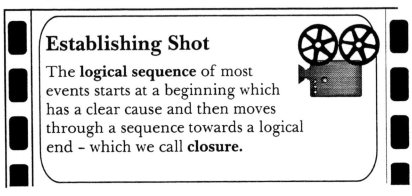

Establishing Shot

The **logical sequence** of most events starts at a beginning which has a clear cause and then moves through a sequence towards a logical end – which we call **closure.**

When events happen out of sequence or do not logically follow each other, or result in an **illogical** ending, then we find the film disjointed and difficult to follow. In extreme cases we might leave the cinema before the end of the film. When the film ends without providing an acceptable ending then we become very aware of our need for loose ends to be tied up, for **closure.** Polanski shows Macbeth "struck withal" by the predictions of the three witches but he closes the film with Donalbain visiting the witches' cave. The ending suggests that Shakespeare's play will be repeated over and over again, that it is timeless. In our desire for closure we can accept this idea, though it is not written in any of the play-texts we have for the play.

The demand for closure is also used to decide whether characters and events are believable. When Petruchio arrives late for his wedding with Katherine (in *The Taming of the Shrew*), we are not surprised because we have been shown his character. We expect him to do something unusual, even bizarre, and we are not disappointed by his lateness or by the strangeness of his costume when he arrives. We are certainly not surprised at Katherine's outrage when he arrives.

Each translation must be read in the context of the time and place the film was made if we are to decide whether our reading is being 'fair' to the film. We cannot expect a film to be read against the historical, cultural and social context it was made in.

The same closure demand also allows us to accept that the shrew, Katherine, may have come to love Petruchio but we expect her to maintain a strong, individual identity. Shakespeare's play-text supports a range of film interpretations which can all suit our demand for a realistic logic.

Shakespeare, Speilberg and Sequels

Modern film-making approaches involve such vast financial outlays that film-makers are continuously seeking ways to increase box office return on their initial capital outlay. As a result, we have seen an increase in merchandising and a conscious effort to see film soundtracks, in particular, as separate commercial products.

A further development in late twentieth century film-making is the tendency to create ambiguous endings where closure is incomplete. The result is the potential for a sequel, a follow-on film which draws on the popularity of the original to sell itself at the box office. Speilberg has been claimed in some quarters as a modern day Shakespeare because of both the diversity and the success of his film-making ventures. Speilberg's approach differs from Shakespeare's, however, in that he often establishes the potential for a sequel to his films by deliberately leaving unresolved elements which can be picked up in future films.

More obvious sequels, like *Rambo* 2, 3, ..., *Terminator* 25, 26, ..., and all of the *Son of* ... Adventures, provide their sequel potential while achieving satisfactory closure by completing an adventure while leaving their central character alive to "fight another day".

Shakespeare, presenting probably only two 'new' plays each summer, needed to create a sense of 'newness' about every play. Some characters, like Sir Toby Belch, were very popular with audiences and they appeared in several different plays. More frequently, however, the need for closure required a strong resolution of all major themes and a sense of completion for the intentions of all major characters. The number of deaths at the close of *Hamlet* suggests one method of achieving this level of closure.

Chapter 13: Hamlet

Establishing Shot

All performances of Shakespeare involve the translation of available play-scripts into performance by live actors. As such, they demand both a reading and a construction of the text. As directors make decisions about staging, costume and setting, they have already begun the process of translation. They may do so in conventional ways, presenting a play in accordance with traditions established over four hundred years of its existence, or they may embark on more radical departures, taking account of contemporary concerns or of whatever else seems most relevant to their producers. The performances of the actors are similarly influenced. All may interpret their characters in a unique way, according to personal or directorial insights; each, however, must read that character in relation to the characters they are playing opposite.

The finished production may choose to emphasise a particular theme at the expense of others. Social violence, incest, arranged marriage, corruption in business are only a few possibilities. Hence a given production may also show a completely different play from that made available in another production. The business of reading a film is always affected by the text presented.

The production choices made by Laurence Olivier (1947), Franco Zeffirelli (1990) and Kenneth Branagh (1996) in their very different presentations of *Hamlet* dramatically illustrate the effects of both reading and constructedness. The much more obscure version from Finland, *Hamlet Goes Business*, directed by Aki Kaurismäki, modernises the play while placing it in the business world in a way similar to the British TV adaptation of *Julius Caesar* (*Heil Caesar*).

Cutaway 13
Take 1

Compare the openings of the Olivier, Zeffirelli and Branagh (four hour version) *Hamlets*. How do they set the tone for what is to follow? What cinematic techniques are most evident and why have they been chosen?

The Domestic Prince

Olivier is very explicit about how he wants his film to be viewed. A voice-over in the opening sequences informs us that "This is the tragedy of a man who could not make up his mind". We first meet a brooding Hamlet, seated a good deal of the time while giving vent to his bitterness about his mother's hasty and incestuous marriage to his uncle within two months of his father's death. A number of the key soliloquies are delivered as voice-overs with Hamlet seated, apparently unsure what to do for the best.

Key Shot– Soliloquy

Spoken alone on stage, the soliloquy usually tells us what the actor is thinking when action cannot reveal it and dialogue would be unsuitable for private thoughts. The film voice-over is similar but need not be the same.

Cutaway 13
Take 2

Hamlet's soliloquies are among the most famous sections of the play. Examine one of them, eg, "To be or not to be", as performed by Olivier, Gibson and Branagh. Which do you admire most from the point of view of an actor's performance? Which do you feel contributes most to a perceptive reading of the play?

Olivier stresses a strongly Oedipal relationship between Hamlet and his mother. Critics have noted the view of Gertrude's empty bed in the opening sequences as being suggestive of a woman's vagina. The bed is prominent in the arras scene when Hamlet kills Polonius. Part of Hamlet's struggle with his mother takes place in and around this same bed. Olivier was forty at the time of the filming and Eileen Herlie, who plays Gertrude, was twenty-seven, so it is probably not surprising that the scene has considerable sexual *frisson* – even when viewed almost half a century later. Zeffirelli's *Hamlet* with Mel Gibson and Glenn Close is even more explicit while Branagh's Hamlet, on the other hand, is not provided with *any* apparent sexual yearnings for his mother. What seem to be simple directorial choices provide us, as film readers, with a range of interpretative options. Their effectiveness becomes a challenge for us as readers and our judgement of the director's choice becomes an issue in our determining the effectiveness of the translation.

Key Shot – Oedipus Complex

In the Greek tragedy by Sophocles, Oedipus killed his father and married his mother. The psychologist Sigmund Freud suggested that it was common for young boys to love their mother and, during early adolescence, to even have sexual feelings toward her. Freud called this the 'Oedipus Complex' and recognised that it was a phase of development which was both normal and, in normally developing boys, relatively brief.

In the final act of the play when Hamlet is duelling with the treacherous Laertes, Olivier's Gertrude views the poisoned cup. A look of recognition on her face, she deliberately drinks from it, against the instructions of the King: "Gertrude, do not drink!". Having realised the extent of the King's plotting, Gertrude appears to sacrifice herself heroically to save her son. But is this a sustainable translation? It appears to rely on Hamlet's love for his mother being returned – even to the death, or is she so disgusted when she realises the true deception of Claudius that she chooses death before a loveless marriage?

To form a reasoned assessment of this translation, it is useful to examine the play-script to see what has been cut and what, if anything, has been added.

What is 'Not' in Olivier's *Hamlet*

Rosencrantz and Guildenstern disappear, as does Fortinbras. The political dimension at both courtly and national levels is also removed. We are given a *Hamlet* that dwells upon the Prince's point of view and his personal dilemmas. Often the shots of what is happening reflect the world as he sees it. Despite its two and a half hours, and in contrast to Parker's *Othello* for example, the film can seem to be rather slow moving by turn-of-the-century standards. The camera's movement to different parts of the castle as the scene changes seems to reflect Hamlet's inactivity.

The omission of Hamlet's friends and acquaintances allows Olivier to establish a 'domestic' *Hamlet* where the deadly tussle between the Prince, his uncle and his mother predominate. This approach denies us a clear view of Hamlet's uncle, now his stepfather, Claudius. In the absence of any other information, we are forced to see Claudius through Hamlet's, possibly quite biased, eyes. Claudius's role as an elder statesman becomes obscured and the wisdom of his independent motivations is hard to read. To provide ourselves with a clearer view of Claudius's motivations, we are well advised to compare the written play-script with Olivier's film translation.

Key Shot –
Who Wrote This Anyway?

Translating *Hamlet*'s play-text is complicated because it exists in three significant variations, the First and Second Quartos and the First Folio. Interestingly, Quarter 1 is usually regarded as a version constructed from the memories of actors by persons wishing to pirate the text; Quarto 2 appeared somewhat hastily in its wake, presumably to correct its errors. Folio 1 was published after Shakespeare's death. None of these texts can be regarded as canonical, ie, as Shakespeare's preferred version – if there ever was such a thing. Producers are free to make whatever use they will of all three play-scripts, and they do. Hence really radical differences can exist between performances of *Hamlet*, usually influenced by producers' and directors' readings of the play.

Hamlet as a Lethal Weapon

Zeffirelli's *Hamlet* is an interesting immediate comparison because in some respects it is clearly influenced by Olivier, while taking a contradictory approach to the Prince. Domesticity prevails and the oedipal relationship between Gertrude and Hamlet is even more obvious. The 40+ years between the two translations allows many on-camera sequences which Olivier could not have sneaked past the censors. Kisses and other demonstrations of physical affection exceed what we might expect between mother and son. The use of the bed is even more passionate. Though Gertrude does not knowingly drink the poison in Act V, Hamlet exchanges a knowing wink with her as he begins to fight Laertes. Is this to impress her with his manly fortitude?

What Zeffirelli does very differently, however, is to reverse Olivier's reading of Hamlet. It was not Mel Gibson's training as a classical actor in Australia that won him the title role, but rather, the impression he made on Zeffirelli as a man of action in *Lethal Weapon*. This Hamlet has more in common with Sylvester Stallone than with Olivier. He is constantly restless and we notice that many speeches are delivered to him and by him when he is on the move. It is as though he can hardly settle long enough to hear what is said to him. This does not preclude his lingering on a parapet to observe what is going on below or pausing to say farewell to his mother as he leaves for England (Zeffirelli's touch is not in the original play-text), but these add further to the sense of action.

Cutaway 13
Take 3

If you were a producer making a film of Hamlet *who would be your ideal choices of actors to play the main roles?*

Why would you choose these actors?

In what ways would this combination of actors be effective in conveying your interpretation of the play?

Hamlet is seen as a man of indecision and inaction in the Olivier translation but in the Zeffirelli translation he seems, more often, to be deciding what he will do next. On board ship he substitutes letters for the ones carried by the sleeping Rosencrantz and Guildenstern. He seems to have guessed the importance of the originals and as we see him reading them, we realise that he had planned the substitution before being certain of what was in the letters.

The inclusion of Rosencrantz and Guildenstern in the Zeffirelli production foregrounds an element of court intrigue which seems to have been deliberately reduced in Olivier's version. It also provides an international context in which Denmark is attached to a wider world. Most notably, however, it provides opportunities for the action hero to demonstrate his abilities. The scene where the two schoolfellows are beheaded becomes less symbolic of the political dependency of England on Denmark than it is of the hero's capacity to be one step ahead of his adversaries and, indeed, to "hoist" them on "their own petard".

Significantly, there is still no sign of Fortinbras in this translation. Instead of opening with the play-script scene on the battlements, Zeffirelli begins with the funeral of old Hamlet to establish the positions of Hamlet, Claudius and Gertrude.

Cutaway 13
Take 4

From Zeffirelli's funeral scene alone, identify the relationships between:

▶ Hamlet and Gertrude

▶ Hamlet and Claudius

▶ Gertrude and Claudius

Explain how these relationships are constructed by the use of camera angle and lighting.

Suggest why Zeffirelli might choose to establish the major characters before he introduces the basis for the story line.

Zeffirelli interpolates speeches and scenes to suit his purpose; eg, parts of Hamlet's nunnery speeches to Ophelia are transposed to our viewing of the film text later than they appear in the play-text. It seems that Zeffirelli is employing the possibilities of the film for greater fluidity than is feasible in a play, and highlighting speeches he wishes highlighted. In doing so, he is able to construct his own interpretation as an experienced and late-century film-maker, the Zeffirelli translation.

Key Shot – The Length of a Play

All productions of Shakespeare use edited and often abridged texts. Whole scenes, events or characters may be left out – or added. Sometimes the action is rearranged. This is particularly necessary with a play like *Hamlet* which takes about four hours if played fully (as in the complete Branagh film version). Most productions are no more than three hours. The play-text prologue of *Romeo and Juliet* states that it will be two hours. Both the Olivier and Zeffirelli films are around two and a half hours and each leaves out major sections of text. In addition, *Hamlet'* textuality is complicated because it exists in three significant variations, the First and Second Quartos and the First Folio.

To Cut or Not to Cut

In Kenneth Branagh's film there is an enhanced sense of size and scope which is partly a result of his using the most complete compilation of play-scripts (and a consequent extra one and a half hours of playing time).

Cutaway 13
Take 5

Kenneth Branagh filmed his *Hamlet* at Blenheim Palace in England and he dressed his characters to the nineteenth century.

Suggest why Branagh might have chosen an English rather than a Danish castle for his setting.

Discuss the effect this information has on your response to the film.

The tone of the Branagh translation is set with the opening, focusing on the title, *Hamlet*. It becomes apparent that this name is carved at the base of the statue of the late King of Denmark. The statue stands before the imposing royal palace, vigilantly guarded by soldiers in the bleak winter landscape.

The statue embodies much that will be important in the story. It is a monument to a recently murdered man whose restless spirit is taking action to induce his son to avenge a wrong. This is the private and personal motivation that will affect young Hamlet. But that man was also a King and his regal importance is apparent when his brother and successor addresses the assembled court. The room is vast and splendid, the courtiers numerous, their dress costly and magnificent. We become aware that this translation is a big budget film with access to the most recent technology and an all-star cast. This knowledge will become part of our reading of the translation when we compare it with the earlier versions – particularly the Olivier translation.

Cutaway 13
Take 6

Since *Hamlet* is a long play, nearly all productions make considerable cuts to the text to reduce playing time to approximately two hours. Compare the Olivier, Zeffirelli and Branagh (two hour version) films of *Hamlet* to determine what sections of the play have been omitted. Consider why the cuts were made. Do they contribute to the success of the film? If you were a producer what sections would you consider essential to your translation? It has been argued that the greater length actually increases the dramatic tension and Branagh's (four hour) translation is the fastest paced of the three films. Is this a reasonable observation?

Claudius's first speech makes reference to the troubled relationship between Denmark and Fortinbras. The dead King was responsible for the death of Fortinbras's father and the King of Norway has had difficulty in restraining his nephew from taking retaliatory action. At various later points in the film there are cutaways to Fortinbras and his troops, ostensibly now merely seeking permission from Denmark to cross its soil to fight the "Polak".

At the end, while Hamlet and Laertes play out their final scene, Fortinbras's troops surround the palace, surprise and overcome the guards and move into the building. As the members of the royal house of Denmark lie recently dead, soldiers crash through the glass doors on all sides while young Fortinbras enters triumphantly from below, somewhat bemused by the carnage that confronts him. He seizes the throne that moments before Hamlet has bequeathed him and is very gracious in his treatment of the body of the Prince. Fortuitously, Fortinbras's transition to power is assisted, though it is unlikely that he would have been baulked by any opposition, and Horatio is left to explain the scene.

Cutaway 13
Take 7

What is your sense of Elsinore as a setting in your reading of this translation of *Hamlet*.

Examine how one film-maker has used the setting in his translation of the play.

Does this use match with your imagined Elsinore?

Does it illuminate or change your sense of the importance of setting in this play?

The film ends with the pomp of Hamlet's funeral and with Fortinbras's soldiers tearing down the statue of old Hamlet. Its head falls in front of the carved name. Unlike Hamlet and Laertes, Fortinbras's dead father is avenged with the fullest possible benefit to the avenger.

Director's Cut 1

Branagh's film provides a much broader historical context than either of the two earlier translations.

Discuss the ways in which Branagh's placement of the Hamlet tragedy within the wider scale suggests that events which seem to be of great importance to the people directly involved may be of little importance in the greater scheme of events.

When Macbeth is told of his wife's death, he observes that

"Life's but a walking shadow, a poor player,
That struts and frets his hour upon the stage,
And then is heard no more: it is a tale
Told by an idiot, full of sound and fury,
Signifying nothing."

Olivier's Hamlet seems closer to Macbeth's observation than Mel Gibson's. Discuss the features of Olivier's translation which suggest that Hamlet is playing a role on a life stage he does not quite understand. Is Branagh's Hamlet "full of sound and fury, signifying nothing"? Or does Fortinbras's success reduce the Hamlet story to yet another "play-within-a-play"?

Intrigue in Court

Fortinbras can be seen as critically important in Branagh's translation because he helps us to see the complexity in Hamlet's view of himself as an avenger. Killing a King is no small task – as both Macbeth and Richard III discover – but killing a king in prayer or asleep may be even harder. Fortinbras has an army to assist him. Branagh's Hamlet is the deeply suspect son of the new King's predecessor. He can expect to be surrounded by the panderers, spies and henchmen of his now stepfather, Claudius. Polonius is the most prominent of these. Polonius can be shown as a prosy old fool but he is shown more importantly by Olivier and Zeffirelli to be single-minded in his scrutiny of Hamlet.

As readers of each translation, we are challenged to decide whether Polonius's interest in Hamlet is best related to his loyalty to his former King, his self-interest as Ophelia's father or his determination as a political survivor to the new king, Claudius. In every case, Hamlet's 'antic disposition' can be seen as a desperate device to take the heat off. Perhaps he hopes that if his actions seem deranged they will seem less threatening to the King, but the Claudius of Branagh's translation is too shrewd to let them pass and he plans to remove Hamlet, initially to England.

Both Zeffirelli's and Branagh's Rosencrantz and Guildenstern are willing tools in Claudius's efforts to scrutinise Hamlet's motivations and control his behaviour. The Prince's initial happiness in seeing his old school friends is quickly tempered when he perceives their real intent. For Branagh though, Claudius's court reflects a political reality which is extended to a national and even international level by young Fortinbras. It is a dangerous place where an insecure, newly installed monarch must be particularly alert to look after his royal person and his newly acquired position.

Gertrude's love for her son and his prominence as Prince are helpful in Claudius's struggle but they are not enough to protect him. Claudius, in every translation, is the ruthless and treacherous murderer of his brother. When matters become really desperate, Branagh's Claudius is quick to notice the same qualities in Laertes and pervert them for his final strike against Hamlet.

The Character of Claudius

In Branagh's four-hour film translation, it is significant that Claudius has a life of his own. He is not simply the incestuous husband of Hamlet's mother nor the lurking murderer that he appears to Hamlet in the other two films. We see more of him away from Hamlet than in the other two productions. As a result, we have more insight into his motivations. He is not just what Alfred Hitchcock called the 'McGuffin' (the excuse for the action) but a substantial figure with his own aspirations and difficulties. He has to deal with the threats of both Hamlet, at home, and Fortinbras, beyond his immediate kingdom, while wishing to enjoy the love of the woman for whom he has sacrificed so much. As his attempt to pray, witnessed but not heard by Hamlet in Branagh's translation, shows, he is more complex than the arrant villain of previous productions.

Claudius knows what he has done and it appears to cause him conflict but he has opted for a worldly course and remains committed to his choice. He is careful in his selection of the instruments who will do his bidding and quick to assess what is afoot. The confrontation between Hamlet and Ophelia that Polonius sets up, and which he witnesses, is an effective ploy from his point of view in establishing just how dangerous the Prince is.

Director's Cut 2

The fullness of Branagh's text allows us insights into Claudius that are denied in the heavily cut previous versions. The use of four hours of cinema opens opportunities for background and character study that are usually only available to us as we read the play-scripts in their various versions – a difficult task for the most dedicated scholars.

Working in small groups, consider how you would support an extended answer to the question:

"Is it reasonable to compare the cinema translations of Olivier and Zeffirelli with the Branagh project of creating a film record of the complete play-script?"

Derek Jacobi's performance displays Claudius as a man of steely nerve with a self-control that underpins his regal dignity. Both qualities have been essential in getting him where he is. In each of the other films, Claudius reacts strongly to the scenario that Hamlet has set up to unmask him. He delivers the line "Give me some light! Away!" in the traditional manner – which seems to leave no doubt that he is shocked and distressed.

While it is equally clear that Jacobi's Claudius is affected, he speaks the line with visible control and contained emotion. He still provides Hamlet and Horatio with the confirmation needed to pursue the Ghost's injunction – but he has not been so easily caught out. Branagh's Claudius is a man whose past success has been achieved through his presence of mind. Because of their substantial shortening, earlier versions necessarily omit these subtleties.

Cutaway 13
Take 9

"The play-within-a-play used to trick Claudius into admitting his killing of the older Hamlet takes time to set up and this time slows the progress of the film. It would be better substituted with a different approach in a modern film version."

Working in small discussion groups, consider the effect of completely removing the play sequence from the Zeffirelli translation.

What effect would this have on Hamlet's decision not to kill Claudius while he is praying?

Would the removal of the play-within-a-play seriously affect Hamlet's motivation in the Olivier translation?

The Avengers: Hamlet and Fortinbras

In Branagh's full film translation, the morally compromising dimensions of the role of the avenger are confronted and interrogated. Hamlet's private vengeance must always have a public aspect. This is equally true for Fortinbras whose righting of the wrong done to his father is played out entirely in the public arena.

On the other hand, Laertes' response to the death of Polonius is motivated completely by personal grievance and leads to the unedifying spectacle of his rushing into the palace at the head of a group of thugs to attack the King. When he is finally appraised of the facts, his feelings are summed up in his willingness to cut Hamlet's "throat i' th' church!" – which seems to suggest that he is more ruthless than Hamlet who had the opportunity to do this to Claudius.

While Laertes becomes a willing contributor to Claudius' plot against Hamlet, his innocent anger contrasts markedly with Hamlet's perception of the impossibility of his own position. He has previously had the opportunity to kill the King at prayer. This location intensifies Hamlet's dilemma about killing Claudius immediately as it recalls the irony of the King's concluding lines:

> *My words fly up, my thoughts remain below:*
> *Words without thoughts never to heaven go.* (III,iii, 97-98)

It also renders more stark Hamlet's decision not to act because if his killing the King were to result in Claudius going to heaven, this would not be revenge. The inactive, frequently seated Hamlet of Olivier's translation can be justified on this point. Hamlet is mindful, of course, that his own father was unshriven and the punishment would not fit the crime. But more starkly, it puts Hamlet into the position of the avenger who must lower himself to the moral level of his victim. It is this moral awareness that makes it so hard for Hamlet to embrace his task, adds to his anguish and generates what the Elizabethan audience would clearly see as a tragic dilemma. Yet it is not merely the ghost's imperative that impels Hamlet to revenge but also his political position. Neither of Branagh's Fortinbras nor Laertes has any trouble with either. Laertes, his father's son, shows little apparent concern for the moral/religious dilemma. Fortinbras sees beyond revenge to an expanded kingdom. Each willingly embraces a part in the corruption he purportedly opposes. Zeffirelli's 'Hamlet-as-Lethal Weapon' does not linger in this dilemma. As a man of action he moves on quickly.

Cutaway 13
Take 10

"Laertes is a minor character with a major role for both Olivier and Zeffirelli." Is this complaint equally true for the four-hour Branagh film?

Hamlet The Lover

Kenneth Branagh's playing of Hamlet reinforces the sense of a man beset with an impossible dilemma. It is not that he is a man who cannot make up his mind; that he cannot be sure what action is appropriate. He is a restless and active figure, fully aware of the dangers of his position and resenting them, quick to sum up the motivations of others, trusting only in Horatio. A poignant example is in his dealings with Ophelia. His love is established in shots of him in bed with her, tenderness a key note in what we are shown. He is at first gentle with her when he meets her in the mirrored hall but as he realises that she is a willing tool of her father and the King who are spying on them through the glass of a double mirror, his fury knows no bounds. Like the presidents, politicians and film stars of today, Hamlet cannot have a personal life in the same way that other people can. The Prince's accuracy of perception is no help in solving his difficulties. He can, at every turn, sum up the situation but he cannot do anything about it. He is Zeffirelli's man of action controlled by Olivier's man who cannot make up his mind.

Cutaway 13
Take 11

Hamlet's love for Ophelia inspires his physical brutality and emotional cruelty. It is not possible for a Prince to love the daughter of a courtier without their love having political implications. Is this a reasonable motive for Hamlet's behaviour towards Ophelia? Discuss Hamlet's response in relation to his duties as a member of the royal family.

Translating and Editing

Each of the three films represents a distinctive translation of Shakespeare's *Hamlet*. Both the choice of text and its presentation are essential elements in our reading. Careful choices are made in the productions to focus attention and shape response. The film medium gives unique opportunities to highlight dramatic moments and to comment on the action. The constructedness of this process becomes clearer when the Olivier and Zeffirelli films are compared with the two-hour version made from Branagh's original. The Branagh version seems less satisfactory than the other two because it is barely half of the original from which it comes. Huge chunks, such as the opening battlement scenes, most of the scenes involving the players and, crucially, the scene of Claudius at prayer, are omitted.

Dissatisfaction for the viewer may come from a close knowledge of the play-script or the uncut four-hour film but it is difficult to remove the impression of a series of excerpts rather than a satisfactory whole. The two-hour version was not conceived as a whole and many of the links and bridges between scenes that could have been made are missing. In contrast, Olivier and Zeffirelli also omit large chunks of the original and remould the characters and their places in the resulting plot to create a new translation. A viewer may or may not be impressed with the result but is more likely to accept its coherence. Inevitably, the play we receive through the film is not only the bard's but someone else's as well. The film is an experience, not of Shakespeare's *Hamlet*, but of Olivier's or Zeffirelli's or Branagh's.

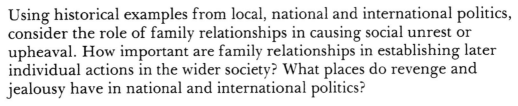

Cutaway 13
Take 12

You are William Shakespeare reincarnated into the late twentieth century. You want to offer guidance to a film director who cannot decide what to cut from the available texts of *Hamlet*. Write director's notes to suggest a film translation you would be pleased to approve for release in Canada, Britain and Australia. Given the opportunity to discuss cutting his four-hour version of *Hamlet* to two hours, prepare the questions you would like to ask Mr Branagh as the screenwriter/director.

Select one of your questions for discussion in your working group and write the answer the group believes Branagh would give to justify his action.

Translation and Cultural Context

Translation must necessarily accept the cultural context into which it is read. Olivier's *Hamlet* was released shortly after the conclusion of the Second Word War. Its success owes much to its audience being able to recognise the survival of the smaller power against overwhelming odds. Zeffirelli's translation followed much lesser engagements such as the Falklands War. His man-of-action has to go out into an unjust world seeking vengeance. Branagh's *Hamlet* followed the first media war, the 'Desert Storm' of the Gulf War with Iraq. Having developed the totality of a film translation in four hours, the cut in which Branagh halves the film length must inevitably remove key motivations, links and even events. Like the media production of the Gulf War – reported every evening on the 6 pm television news – and the confused reporting of the actions of Serbs, Croats, Albanians and Moslems in the former Jugoslavia, Branagh's two-hour *Hamlet* leaves us slightly dissatisfied. Have we really understood the action? Do we really know why it is happening? Do we even understand who the key players are – or what they really stand for?

Cutaway 13
Take 13

One of the stated reasons for continuing to study Shakespeare's plays is that their themes are timeless.

Using historical examples from local, national and international politics, consider the role of family relationships in causing social unrest or upheaval. How important are family relationships in establishing later individual actions in the wider society? What places do revenge and jealousy have in national and international politics?

Further Possibilities for Discussion

❖ Compare the scene involving Hamlet, Polonius and Gertrude in her bedroom as it is shown by Olivier, Zeffirelli and Branagh. What do you learn from this scene about (a) the translation of *Hamlet* given in the film, (b) the relationships of the three characters in the play as a whole?

❖ Olivier plays Hamlet as a man of inaction; Gibson plays him as a man of action; Branagh plays him as a sensitive man enmeshed in a world of political intrigue. How is it possible for such widely variant renderings of the same character to appear on film? Is it reasonable to claim any one of these performances is more authentically Shakespearean than the others? Establish detailed reasons for your view.

❖ What advantages does a good film of *Hamlet* offer as distinct from a stage production? Are there any disadvantages?

❖ In a film, pieces of "business" not in the original play-text can be crucial to the view of the play the audience is being given. Examine some examples of such business in any of the films of *Hamlet* you have seen. How do they contribute to the producer's interpretation of the play?

❖ Zeffirelli's *Hamlet* is medieval in appearance, Olivier's roughly contemporary with Shakespeare. Branagh places the film in a more recent period. In what ways are our responses to the film guided by these factors?

❖ Does Olivier's *Hamlet* gain or lose by being in black and white?

Chapter 14:
Romeo and Juliet

Establishing Shot

Numerous attempts have been made to film *Romeo and Juliet*. Only four have been considered as serious film interpretations of the play. The most acceptable to teachers and, later, to scholars, has been the 1968 Zeffirelli version which gained critical acclaim for its use of 16 and 17 year old actors to play the title roles. In sharp contrast, the 1929 version directed by George Cukor starred Leslie Howard and Norma Shearer (both established and popular film stars but 43 and 36 respectively at the time of filming – rather difficult to accept as teenagers). The 1954 version directed by Renato Castellani starred Lawrence Harvey (aged 26) and Susan Shantall (aged 20 in her only film). The most immediately popular film translation has been the recent 1996 Luhrmann version which quickly captured the imagination of teenage audiences, many of whom have seen the film multiple times without urging. This chapter will focus on the reading of particular sections and thematic issues from the readily available treatments of Baz Luhrmann and Franco Zeffirelli.

Acknowledging The Source

While scholars continue to discuss the authorship of Shakespeare's plays, it is clear that each was actually presented by Shakespeare's company of actors – though possibly never in the form we now have as the published play script. It is generally accepted that the plays were probably never written down in their entirety while they were being performed; that they changed according to who was playing particular roles and that they changed according to audience response and identity.

Documentary evidence suggests that *Romeo and Juliet* was probably developed as a play by Shakespeare's company in 1594 or 1595. Like many of the Elizabethan plays, it is based on stories popular at the time and known to the intended audience. Being set in Italy, it cannot be said to be talking about current events in England and its location, for the audience, is both exotic and, at the time, popular.

In his title sequence, Zeffirelli acknowledges the play as his production of William Shakespeare's *Romeo and Juliet*. Luhrmann takes this acknowledgement one step further and titles his film *William Shakespeare's 'Romeo and Juliet'*. The acceptance by each director that he is working with material first developed by another author provides him with an excuse for modifying the script but suggests that each has a clear understanding of the text he is working from.

Zeffirelli's setting of *Romeo and Juliet* in Verona accepts the historical and geographic locations provided by the play-text. As a result, we expect Shakespearean language and, where it is not made redundant by visual access to costume, properties and scenery, Elizabethan manners and conventions. In stark contrast, Luhrmann has reinterpreted both time and place while maintaining the language of the play-text. The resulting film provides us with access to modern day characters speaking in a rather strange dialect of English. For some viewers this tends to create a tension between audience and production that forces a concentration on listening for meaning rather than watching for action. The effect is similar to viewing an Australian film in Canada or vice versa.

Director's Cut 1

It has been argued that because Luhrmann's version of *William Shakespeare's Romeo and Juliet* requires close listening to the language and is presented in modern dress in a contemporary setting, it is a more accurate production of Shakespeare's intention than Zeffirelli's. Using the findings of your research into the way Elizabethan theatre was used as an entertainment, consider the validity of this argument.

Film as a Product of its Historical Setting

In the late 1960s, major media concerns revolved around the continuing battles between teenage gangs in Britain and the increase in draft dodging and anti-Vietnam involvement in America. The musical impact of the Beatles on teen culture equalled the impact of the protest songs of Bob Dylan; the American National Guard had shot students protesting on campuses at Kent State in Ohio and at Berkeley in California. The President of the United States, John Kennedy, had been assassinated and so had the African-American civil-rights leader, Martin Luther King, Jr. Parental guidance of children and challenges to traditional family values of obedience and subservience had come into question following widespread acceptance of a book on parenting by Dr Benjamin Spock.

When Zeffirelli directed *Romeo and Juliet,* the rights of Church and State were in question from the generation born after the Second World War. The age when childhood became adulthood was in serious dispute from young people likely to be conscripted to fight a war they did not understand on behalf of leaders they were unwilling to trust. The issues and themes which underlie the core of *Romeo and Juliet* were the focus of the generation.

Two generations later, and shortly after the Gulf War, which is widely accepted as the first war ever completely stage-managed for the media, Luhrmann directed a media-focused version of the same play. Again, many of the major concerns of the media had been focused around family values and authority appearing to have been rejected by the younger generation. Historically responsive to the times, Luhrmann's interpretation is set within a decaying social structure where appearance is more important than substance, drug-dependent teenage gangs apparently hold the streets to ransom, sexuality is at least ambiguous in the face of the AIDS epidemic and the simple values of love and forgiveness seem, again, to have been lost forever.

Cutaway 14
Take 1

It has been argued that "The film version of a play can only reflect the values established within the play". *Romeo and Juliet* appears to be a play which can reflect its values through any place and any period.

To what extent is any film interpretation of a play a construction of its director and screenwriters?

Opening the Film

Despite their vastly different approaches to film-making and to their interpretation of the play-script, both Zeffirelli and Luhrmann open their films with the prologue from the original play as a voice-over.

The Prologue [enter Chorus]

Chorus

Two households, both alike in dignity,
In fair Verona, where we lay our scene,
From ancient grudge break to new mutiny,
Where civil blood makes civil hands unclean.
From forth the fatal loins of these two foes
A pair of star-cross'd lovers take their life;
Whose misadventur'd piteous overthrows
Do with their death bury their parents' strife.
The fearful passage of their death-mark'd love,
And the continuance of their parents' rage
Which, but their children's end, naught could remove,
Is now the two hours' traffick of our stage;
The which if you with patient ears attend,
What here shall miss, our toil shall strive to mend.

[exit]

Zeffirelli's camera pans slowly from fog and smog across the outline of Verona beneath a weak and wintry sun before it zooms in to the town square. Luhrmann zooms slowly in to a television set on which a Hispanic female newscaster is broadcasting details of the latest street riots in a more modern but depressed, and apparently American, Verona. As Luhrmann cuts to street scenes, viewers familiar with the play become quickly aware that billboards and hoardings carry quotes from the play-text.

Cutaway 14
Take 2

The Luhrmann title sequence introduces the characters in a mixture of media 'hype' and more subtle information giving. The characters are named in identifiable and contemporary terms as their roles are established.

Working as a newspaper columnist, watch the credits through and then attempt to write a brief background article in which you introduce the major characters, their roles and their relationships with each other.

Discuss the effectiveness of Luhrmann's title sequence in providing an understanding of the setting, the plot and the key players.

Compare the effectiveness of Luhrmann's title sequence with that of Zeffirelli. What has Zeffirelli gained and what has he lost from using a more conventional film opening?

The Shakespearean audience was used to listening rather than viewing. In fact, before the audience settled, many may not have been able to see the chorus delivering the prologue. What information is provided by Zeffirelli's title sequence which is not available in the prologue of the play?

Luhrmann's camera watches the opening scene unfold from above and afar – even clinically. As events unfold, we are close enough to note the detail but we remain far away enough to feel protected from the violence of the action. We see the guns, the looks on faces, the detail around the doorways and in the advertising signs. It is familiar but not identical with our own environment. We anticipate the flames which end the scene and maybe even hope that the police will intervene.

In contrast, Zeffirelli takes his camera down into the square, among the stalls and between the feet of the vendors and buyers. As a result, we look up to the Capulets and the Montagues from our first viewing. We note their contrasting colours, their swaggering walks. As intimates in the marketplace, we are involved in the action, the insult and the ensuing scuffle. We retreat with the camera as the Prince and his guard arrive. We are among the 'enemies of peace' and we feel the threat that our 'lives shall pay the forfeit of the peace'.

Casting the Title Roles

In settings owing more to opera and ballet than Shakespeare's play-text, Zeffirelli presents an almost unbelievably romantic Romeo [Leonard Whiting] and a childishly naive Juliet [Olivia Hussey]. The introduction of Romeo with soulfully darkened eyes and flowers in hand borrows heavily on the black-and-white make-up style of romantic film stars from the 1920s such as Rudolph Valentino or Mary Pickford. To teenage audiences in the late 1990s, it makes Romeo an unlikely leader among the young Montagues, and suggests that Juliet would be too innocent to fall in love at first sight.

Unlikely as the romance seems, however, Zeffirelli effectively distances the world of romance from the harsh reality of civil strife. The result allows for meaningful observation of Juliet's family at home and some significant identification of the problems associated with arranged marriage. In contrast, it provides for a similar exploration of the depth of the family feuding.

Luhrmann's version, filmed in Mexico, is most obviously a product of the media generation. The frenetic street violence of the large city is watched over by a gigantic statue of Christ, its arms outstretched, while the helicopters of law enforcement transcend even the power of the Church by buzzing around it like angry insects.

Like Zeffirelli, Luhrmann casts for youth though both Romeo (Leonardo di Caprio) and Juliet (Clare Dane) are somewhat more worldly-wise and possibly more credible in their context than Zeffirelli's 'star-cross'd lovers'. The consequence of this choice is a loss of family intimacy in the Capulet household. Luhrmann's Lady Capulet has more in common with an image-infatuated social-climbing shrew than with the embittered mother of seven dead children who thinks that her only surviving child is to be wed on her husband's orders at age 14.

Cutaway 14
Take 3

The huge statue of the Christ is first seen in the title sequence of Luhrmann's film. Its representation of the power of the Church over the lives of the people below is overshadowed by the way the police and media helicopters move above and around it. Zeffirelli's more traditional Church is across the square from the entry through which the Prince's guard move to stop the riot begun by the thumb-biting insult.

Discuss the effectiveness of the two approaches in separating and then highlighting the relative powers of Church and State in the film versions.

In what ways are the two versions different from any portrayal that might have been permitted in Shakespeare's times?

Design an alternative approach to establishing the difference between Church and State powers taking advantage of the interpretations of current events influencing world leaders and their families for a film version to be released in 2003.

The Arranged Marriage

Zeffirelli casts Juliet's suitor, Paris, as an old man – perhaps 60, possibly even older. The potential mismatch with the thirteen-year-old Juliet is stark, even horrifying in many western societies. Capulet's warning that there is much grief in marrying too young is highlighted as the camera looks over his shoulder to his embittered wife. Her age is uncertain but she also was married young, as Capulet tells Paris, and has been married at least 14 years. She could be as young as 27, probably not older than 38. Capulet is at least 60 so Paris is relatively even older in seeking marriage with Juliet. We never know whether he has been married before – his wife/wives may have died in childbirth.

As Luhrmann focuses on the media opportunities flowing from the family feud, he creates a frenetic world of fast-cut editing where law enforcement is more threatening than family traditions and where the playboy Paris, Verona's 'most eligible bachelor of the year', is unlikely to be arranging to wed a thirteen-year-old. The brief discussion between Paris and Capulet adds little to our understanding of the unfolding events though it provides a showcase for Lady Capulet's socialite hysteria while debasing the role of the nurse in Juliet's upbringing.

Cutaway 14
Take 4

Using a copy of the play-text, find the scene in which Paris speaks with Capulet about the possibility of marriage with Juliet. Consider the scene as a director. Is the scene important? Considering the likely ages of Juliet and her parents, discuss the possibility of leaving the scene out of the film. How would this affect the following scene with Lady Capulet, the Nurse and Juliet?

Masque

On a dramatic level, the Capulet's masked ball is a simple device for allowing Romeo to meet Juliet. From an entertainment perspective, it probably provided the original Elizabethan audience with an opportunity to watch an equivalent of "Lives of the Rich and Famous". Its lengthy prologue sequence, where Mercutio makes fun of Romeo as a dreamer, allows Luhrmann to extend his use of the mood enhancing drugs as a method of reducing inhibition. The introduction of drugs is consistent with Luhrmann's interpretation of the play but the introduction of the Queen Mab story to explain dreams and dreamers seems irrelevant in this context.

Romeo's cat mask in the Luhrmann film can be seen in a number of ways but when Tybalt describes himself as the "King of cats", the antagonism between the two families is refocused. Tybalt sees Romeo at the ball and tells his father to have the Montagues removed. Capulet refuses and Tybalt's hatred is boundless. Through use of the Masque, Luhrmann provides a stronger motivation for the later fight than Zeffirelli – though both tend to use it as a musical interlude from the violence. The families can, in fact, co-exist within the formalities of a clear social framework – which the Prince has given them. More significantly, with or without masks, if the family name tags are removed, Romeo and Juliet can fall in love like any young people.

Cutaway 14
Take 5

Using your understanding of the characters of Tybalt and Mercutio, design and create masks suitable for them to wear at the Capulet Masque.

Using your research findings, discuss the use of masque and suggest whether it would be an effective disguise in a real situation.

Suggest why Shakespeare might have included the masque within the play and explore alternatives which could have been used by each of the film-makers under discussion.

The Theatre of War

The 'play within a play' structure which is commonly used to allow parallel actions to develop is not a feature of the play-text of *Romeo and Juliet*. However, the need to separate the reality of the family feud from the romance of the title characters requires a recognition of the differences between reality and fantasy.

Mercutio's cross-dressed performance as a nightclub entertainer blurs the lines defining sexuality in Luhrmann's film. Romeo's actions, his speech, his manner and, in Zeffirelli's version, his make-up and flower-carrying each suggest that he is more comfortable with his masculinity than with the male role he is expected to play.

Luhrmann's headquarters for the Montague gang, the stage of a wrecked cinema, is defined by the remaining proscenium arch. The auditorium has been demolished, there is no shelter, the projection box has gone and the screen itself has been removed. Instead of a filmic fantasy, the gang sees reality – almost always stormy and usually at sunset. Ultimately, both Tybalt and Mercutio fall from the stage. Tybalt falls through the screen area, out of the theatre. Mercutio dies in the auditorium area, in the theatre of war.

Zeffirelli's approach, in some ways, is even more bleak. Neither gang is located in a stable environment. They meet together in the streets, they play on the steps of the Church and at the well but never enter any of the buildings. They climb narrow lanes and pass through arches but only Tybalt is ever at home [during the masque]. Even then his home is invaded and he is helpless to respond.

Cutaway 14
Take 6

Luhrmann's film seems to provide or suggest many places for the gangs to meet. Zeffirelli's film seems too neat to allow a space. Sometimes it seems too clean and orderly for the tragedy to develop.

Use your research findings to design areas which could have been used by Zeffirelli to create spaces for the gangs to meet amongst themselves. Develop your findings as set drawings and models.

The Play as Social Commentary and Satire

It is usual to describe *Romeo and Juliet* as a tragedy resulting from a family feud. The prologue states that the play lasts for two hours, that it will show the deaths of two young people who fell in love and that their families would not stop feuding until their deaths. More importantly, perhaps, the prologue asks the audience to listen carefully and promises that what they do not understand from hearing, they will be able to see in the action on stage.

The tone of the prologue suggests that the play will present a lesson to the audience. It seems unlikely, however, that an Elizabethan audience would walk to the theatre to stand watching an entertainment for two hours, possibly in the rain, if they were to be the target for a lesson in family politics. The play would be expected to present more conscious entertainment so it is worth considering alternative interpretations.

The relationship between the Catholic Queen Mary (known as 'Bloody Mary'; Queen 1553-1558) and her Protestant sister, Queen Elizabeth I (1558-1603), forms an historical background for the play so the Capulets and Montagues might represent the 'families' of Catholic and Protestant believers. This interpretation would be dangerous for Shakespeare and his company if either group objected to the portrayal.

A number of playwrights were imprisoned – some for long terms – for treason because they hinted criticism of the Crown, the State or the Church in their works. This law was finally rescinded in the 1970s!

The prologue states from its first line that the two households are 'both alike in dignity'. To be safe, however, the play concentrates its attention on the children of the families rather than their parents. In doing so, it allows the adults to avoid criticism. Adults, when they are able to distance themselves from the action, usually accept that young people may show their ignorance, engage in silly actions and over-react to adult emotions. The action in *Romeo and Juliet* can be seen as a satire on children growing up. Even more importantly, as is usual in Shakespeare's plays, it can be seen as a satire on the actions and excesses of the 'rich and shameless', the nobility, people in power in far away places – this time Italy.

In satirising the adolescent children of the nobility, Shakespeare provides a platform from which to explore serious issues of parenting together with serious issues of government. Juliet's age is discussed by Paris and Capulet in relation to her child-bearing. Capulet dismisses her physical ability to bear children at age 13 and considers, instead, the effect of multiple child-bearing and loss on the relationship between husband and wife. He suggests that Paris should wait at least until Juliet is sixteen. In different contexts – *The Taming of the Shrew* and *Merry Wives of Windsor* – similar discussions become the source of obvious humour. Zeffirelli foregrounds the theme of age readiness for marriage as he foregrounds the role of the nurse in mothering Juliet. The resulting scenes of farce provide a clear indication of the potential for satire within the play. Luhrmann, on the other hand, reduces these scenes to the point where the nurse becomes little more than a regularly abused messenger – first for Lady Capulet and then for Juliet.

The role of the Church in assisting Juliet to marry Romeo remains difficult to interpret. It cannot be omitted because the pair need a 'safe house' to meet in. Friar Lawrence is seen as an alchemist by both Zeffirelli and Luhrmann. Luhrmann is more pointed in suggesting that the priest is developing and distributing drugs and, furthermore, teaching the next generation [of choirboys] how to do likewise. He is presented as an ambiguous character, possibly wishing to help but apparently warped in his intention. Under his guidance, Romeo is presented as a spaced-out hero to the younger boys.

Fagan in *Oliver Twist* fills a similar role in saving Oliver from starvation but placing him in greater danger by training him as a thief – who will be imprisoned or even hanged if he is caught. In this parallel, Romeo appears to be the Artful Dodger.

Zeffirelli's Friar is a slightly more innocent character, a well-intentioned creature of the night who tries to do the right thing for Juliet but mucks up. Either interpretation would suit Shakespeare's purpose in suggesting that the interference of the Church in England was causing suffering to the 'children of the Church'.

The events leading to the tragedy in which Juliet wakes to find that Romeo has committed suicide because he thought that she was already dead and so she commits suicide too, border on high farce. In both film interpretations, the camera succeeds in presenting compelling images but it remains among the weakest scenes. The deathbed speeches are powerful but they are the speeches of children who cannot understand that they have over-reacted to create their own tragedies. Zeffirelli allows the closing sequences to generate their own power and, for adult audiences, these are quite effective. Adolescent audiences are less forgiving and the High-camp ending of Luhrmann is more satisfying because it admits the farcical nature of the sequence. The church is more highly lit than for a coronation, the corpse of Juliet is effectively enthroned in virginal white and the finger-twitching of Juliet's 'almost in time' recovery provides an acceptance of the melodrama which is confirmed when the camera cranes out to view the sanitised set-piece ending – the corpses carefully arranged across each other and a carefully arranged spattering of blood.

What do you think would be the most effective way of presenting the play-text to a present day film or television audience?

Further Possibilities for Discussion

1. Life after Romeo

It is a simple matter to suggest that both Romeo and Juliet died for their love of each other but this is a very unsatisfactory resolution to a more complex play. In fact, it is this interpretation which makes the play so difficult to present credibly. Romeo and Juliet have sought refuge in the Church. They have been married in the Church and their upbringing would have steeped them in the laws of the Church. It is unlikely, under these circumstances, that suicide would have been seen as the immediate solution to their problems.

Juliet deliberately, and under the guidance of her priest, fakes suicide to avoid marriage to a man she does not love – Paris. Luhrmann's film interpretation indicates that Romeo, already banished from Verona for his killing of Tybalt, accepts that his wife has committed suicide and therefore, grief stricken, has nothing to lose by joining her. Zeffirelli does not make this link so clearly.

When Juliet wakes to find that Romeo has taken his life from grief, she would appear to have several alternatives to suicide. Both Shakespeare and the film-makers, however, have already exhausted several of these.

If Juliet had not faked suicide, she might have returned to her family, begged forgiveness and married Paris. For both Zeffirelli and Luhrmann, this alternative has been eliminated in their decision to make an explicit scene of the consummation of the marriage.

If Juliet had gone to the Montagues, told them she had married Romeo and that the marriage had been consummated, she could beg their forgiveness and live with them. Unfortunately, Romeo's banishment and, more particularly, his suicide make this an impossible option because she is now the only living focus of the hatred between the families.

If Juliet went away quietly, everyone could forget the tragic events and she could enter a nunnery.

What other possibilities exist for saving Juliet from suicide?

Suggest why both Shakespeare and the film-makers have accepted the multiple suicide ending although it goes against the teaching of the Roman Catholic Church.

2. Music

Music is used cleverly and constantly by both Zeffirelli and Luhrmann to extend the mood of the play and to develop relationships without the need for additional dialogue. The theme from Zeffirelli's *Romeo and Juliet* won an Oscar for Nino Rota. The central entertainment at Zeffirelli's masque is the song that foreshadows the ending, 'So dies the youth/So dies the fairest maid'. Luhrmann portrays Mercutio as a nightclub entertainer and several of the sequences depend on his talent as an entertainer.

West Side Story presents an extreme example of the use of music by interpreting the play as a stage musical. The filmed version of the musical is readily available on videotape and provides a challenging extension of the concept of translation from one entertainment form to another.

Consider the use of music by each film-maker at critical points in the story. How does the different interpretation of each director provide him with options unavailable from the play-text?

3. Courtship and marriage

Although several of the issues associated with the marriage of Romeo and Juliet can be equally discussed by reference to the play-text alone, reference to the filmed interpretations helps us towards a powerful understanding of:

❖ the role of the nurse in Juliet's upbringing – and in her death;

❖ the place of the arranged marriage in Elizabethan society and, in some modern societies at differing social levels.

Consider how the changing times during which the film translations of *Romeo and Juliet* have been completed have allowed their directors to extend the meaning of parenting available from the play-text.

4. The family feud

❖ *Romeo and Juliet* contains some of the best Elizabethan insults available from Shakespeare's play-texts. Identify the insults, discuss how they are supposed to work and consider whether the nature of the insult has been changed by each of the film-makers.

❖ Gang warfare is presented quite differently by Zeffirelli and Luhrmann: the musical *West Side Story* provides a further alternative. Consider whether the social commentary on gang warfare is as important as the expression of tragedy for the lovers and suggest an alternative translation in which Romeo and Juliet become minor characters in the production. Suggest a name for your new film and identify the lead characters.

❖ If Capulet had evicted the Montagues from the Masque, Romeo would not have met Juliet and the tragedy could have been avoided. It is Capulet's treatment of Tybalt that moves the action from civil unrest to tragedy. Do you agree?

Chapter 15: Further Opportunities for Discussion

Establishing Shot

The recent film *Shakespeare in Love* presents a very amusing suggestion about how *Romeo and Juliet* came to be written and performed. Co-written by Tom Stoppard (who also wrote *Rosencrantz and Guildenstern are Dead* – a derivative from *Hamlet*), the film provides excellent background about the life and times of young William Shakespeare. At the same time, it introduces Christopher Marlowe, John Webster and a range of the essential names associated with Elizabethan theatre in a highly entertaining context.

The Ensemble and Authorship

One of the assumptions behind the writing of much of this book is the belief that the actual writing of "Shakespeare's play-scripts" was never undertaken by Shakespeare. Instead, as the company owner and director, Shakespeare suggested the ideas and probably wrote major speeches which were needed to fit particular sections of each play. Using this belief, we can suggest that the reason for the folio and quarto versions of the Shakespeare plays was to record what people thought were memorable events so that they could be played again – much as we buy the videotape of a film or series so that we can watch it again at our leisure.

Like the audience for the Greek and Roman plays, the Elizabethan audience already knew most of the stories they were seeing on the stage. Like today's audiences, they were familiar with previous kings and queens, battles and romances. They were familiar with the probable intrigues and gossip that always surrounds famous people and, like modern audiences, they liked to see plays about what goes on between the rich and famous.

With this belief, it seems quite acceptable that every generation should remake its own translations of the Shakespeare plays in the medium that is most accessible and entertaining for them at the time. The theatre was the only available place to see organised entertainment until the invention of moving pictures. The cinema still required us to travel out of our homes to see the entertainment though, for the first time, the actors did not have to travel to the same theatre to present their entertainment. Television is the first medium which has allowed us to view organised entertainment in our own homes.

The value of considering Shakespeare's plays as the result of an ensemble of actors working together to develop an entertainment is that it allows us to see why different folios contain different texts, why there do not seem to be any remnants of Shakespeare's play-scripts written in his own hand and why some of the lines could not have been delivered more than once in an Elizabethan theatre (consider the reference to a camel-shaped cloud in an open air theatre).

Tom Stoppard, who provided the idea and co-wrote the screenplay for *Shakespeare in Love*, has been threatened with law suits for taking his ideas, and much of the action and dialogue, from an earlier play. The approach is truly Shakespearean. If it is a good play and a good idea then it should be seen and heard. Unfortunately, the concept of authorship is far more rigid in our own time than it was 300 years ago.

The role of the printing press has played a large part in hardening our ideas of who wrote what. Despite the work of editors and publishers in influencing writers to meet commercial demands or social expectations, the author of a printed work is considered to be a simply identifiable person or group of persons. The complexity of film-making, however, makes it difficult to attribute the authorship to any single member of the vast team who work on the production. Screenwriters, directors, producers, actors and even sponsors may all shape the wording as much as the interpretation. Editors, similarly, create subtle differences which may create entirely different readings by sequencing shots to match the demands of music, sound and dialogue.

Shakespeare in Love shows Christopher Marlowe giving Shakespeare an idea for a play, the leading actor agreeing to take a smaller part because it better fits the needs of the story and accidental business on stage being included because it works. *Shakespeare in Love* provides some very useful possibilities for the interpretation and understanding of both Shakespearean play-scripts and Elizabethan times.

Voice as Identity

❖ Highly successful Hollywood actors have frequently had distinctive voices. Part of the benefit of a distinctive voice is that the public recognises the actor from film to film. This may be seen as an aid to building star status. A second advantage of distinctive voices is that they help the audience to keep the characters straight, especially in productions with large casts. Of course, there are other ways of helping the audience to keep the characters straight: the use of similarly coloured costumes for the members of each clan (for example, the Montagues and the Capulets); and the liberal use of characters' names by other characters. List other methods that directors use to help audiences to remember who is who.

Some of the actors in these productions may be recognizable to you through their voices. Choose actors from the play whose voices you recognise from other films or television productions. List these actors and actresses and the other work they have appeared in. Working with others in your study group, create a poster which shows a picture of the actor and lists her or his film credits. Describe ways in which the actor's voice is distinct. Include a cassette tape of her or his voice from at least two other productions.

❖ Make a list of famous movie actors who have distinctive voices. Include as many movies and roles as you can. Compare your list with those of others in your study group. Make a poster. Include a cassette tape with examples of their voices and see if others recognise the voices on tape.

Directors

❖ Biographies of such famous directors as Alfred Hitchcock and Sir Laurence Olivier offer interesting insights into the visions of film directors and the ways they present them. Evan Hunter's *Me and Hitch* and Jon Tuska's *Encounters with Film-makers: Eight Career Studies* demonstrate the ways directors and producers contribute to the vision presented in films. Research the biographical details of the director of one of your favourite films. In a paragraph, outline the vision the director presents in the film. Cite evidence which shows either how the director came to this vision or which presents a similar or complementary vision. Write a review of the film describing the director's vision and introducing biographical data to support your position.

Cultural Capital

❖ Parents and neighbours can be rich sources of folklore about characteristics associated with the birth order of children. Collect some of the lore surrounding birth order and compare it with information available from basic psychology books and parenting magazines. Is Goneril a typical oldest child? Is Cordelia a typical youngest? Pay particular attention to attributes of the middle child of three, Regan's position in her family. Discuss the likely response of a Shakespearean audience to Regan's actions during a performance of the play. Suggest how these reactions would affect a modern interpretation of Regan for a film production.

❖ How important is it to have read the play-text before you can appreciate the film translation? What advantages are there in being familiar with the quotable quotes from a play before you watch the film translation?

Film Reviews/Book Reviews/Arts Reviews

❖ Critics of the arts (drama, film, art, music, literature, etc) can help readers, viewers and audiences to understand and appreciate aesthetic works. Some people read the critics' opinions before deciding whether or not to attend or view or read a work. More often we read the critics following our experience of the work to compare their opinions with ours. Locate at least two reviews of one film translation of a recent Shakespearean play or movie and compare the reviewers' responses with your own. Write a review which presents and supports your opinions while acknowledging the opinions of the other reviewers.

Suicide

Despite being a Catholic in a Catholic country where suicide is a mortal sin, Juliet feels that she has no option but suicide because she has offended her own parents and married into a family who are sworn enemies. Othello does not seem to have any particular religious beliefs but takes his own life because he believes he has failed in his expectations of himself as a man.

Research the attitudes to suicide and to responsibilities between man and wife in Elizabethan society. Use your findings to suggest how Shakespeare was able to use suicide as a method of closing two of his tragedies.

Murder

Murder is used variously in Shakespeare's plays to provide motivations for revenge, to remove unwanted characters from the scene and to offer insights into the desperation of characters to achieve their goals.

In Polanski's *Macbeth*, the murder of King Duncan sends the crown spinning across the floor symbolising social chaos. Identify one play in which murder is central to the plot and establish how the film-maker has established the importance of the murder by the use of visual symbolism. Discuss the success of the scene in setting the tone of the film for the action that follows.

Childbirth and Early Survival

Juliet is the only surviving child from her parents' marriage – which helps to explain their reactions to Paris. Lady Macbeth speaks of the child to whom she has 'given suck' as she works herself up to the murder of Duncan. (But no child is referred to elsewhere – so perhaps it has died; which might explain why she is so bitter.) Hamlet seems to be the only child of his father though we do not know how many times Hamlet senior may have married (one reason for Glenn Close to be the same age as Mel Gibson in the Zeffirelli version).

Early childhood diseases, death in childbirth and stillbirth are not dwelt on in Shakespeare's play-texts but they are commonly mentioned and form one argument for the marriage of very young women to older men. Shakespeare appears to have discussed this matter in a number of plays, suggesting that women should be older before they marry.

Use your research into Shakespeare's life and marriage to suggest why this should be a recurring theme in play-texts where there is no other motive for their appearance.

Satires, Spoofs and Commercial Cinema

Shakespeare's play-texts have become increasingly popular subjects for film during the past thirty years. The most recent series of film translations have covered the histories, comedies and tragedies in a range of innovative ways, some more successfully than others.

Shakespeare in Love is a delightful representation of what, most likely, was **not** the origin of *Romeo and Juliet*. Instead, it suggests that Shakespeare was one of a number of producers, playwrights and actors all seeking attention in Elizabethan London. It plausibly suggests that some of the famous lines, especially the insults, were everyday sayings. Most importantly, it provides its viewers with a romantically realistic context in which to read and hear Elizabethan text.

Discuss the importance of the commercialisation of Shakespeare for the reading and interpretation of his play-texts. Identify the insights you have gained into Shakespeare's world from viewing *Shakespeare in Love*.

Just as Shakespeare collected his plots from history, from popular stories and from current events of his time, Shakespeare's play-texts have presented modern day film-makers with plots for films which explore the issues without clinging to the language, the poetry of the detail.

❖ *Forbidden Planet* provided a launching pad for translating *The Tempest* to outer space.

❖ *Joe Macbeth* brought *Macbeth* to America as a gangster.

❖ *Kiss me Kate* became a musical version of *Taming of the Shrew* while *West Side Story* was the musical version of *Romeo and Juliet*

❖ *Hamlet* went west in 1972 as *Johnny Hamlet*.

❖ *Henry IV* became *Chimes at Midnight* for Orson Welles

❖ *King Lear* went west and was modernised in *A Thousand Acres*.

❖ *China Girl* brought a Chinese Juliet to New York to meet her Italian Romeo in a mafia-dominated Little Italy.

❖ In *Prospero's Books*, Peter Greenaway threw a little *Tempest* to create a cinematic wonderland for the Duke of Milan's revenge and a showcase for John Gielgud's voice, not to mention large scenes of nudity for late-night TV.

What other translations or borrowings from Shakespeare's plays can you discover? Discuss the effectiveness of any of these you have the opportunity to view.

Use one of the Shakespearean plays you have studied to create a film scenario that would be appealing to a present day audience. Make specific notes of: the cuts you have made; the changes in time and place; any changes in relationships which help to enhance the plot or intensify the themes.

References

Film

Broken Lance (1954), director Edward Dmytryck.
Bullitt (1968), director Peter Yates.
China Girl (1987), director Abel Ferrara.
Forbidden Planet (1956), director Fred M Wilcox.
Hamlet (1948), director Lawrence Olivier.
Hamlet (1969), director Tony Richardson.
Hamlet (1991), director Franco Zeffirelli.
Hamlet (1998), director Kenneth Branagh.
Joe Macbeth (1955), director Ken Hughes.
King Lear (1953), directors Peter Brook and Andrew McCullough.
King Lear (1969), director Peter Brook.
King Lear (1984), director Michael Elliott.
Macbeth (1972), director Roman Polanski.
Men of Respect (1990), director William Reilly.
A Midsummer Night's Dream (1999), director Michael Hoffman.
Othello (1951), director Orson Welles.
Othello (1965), director Stuart Burge.
Othello (1986), director Franco Zeffirelli.
Othello (1995), director Oliver Parker.
Propero's Books (1991), director Peter Greenaway.
RAN (1985), director Akiro Kurosawa.
Richard III (1955), director Lawrence Olivier.
Richard III (1996), director John Loncraine.
Romeo and Juliet (1968), director Franco Zeffirelli.
Romeo and Juliet (1997), director Baz Luhrmann.
Shakespeare in Love (1998), director John Madden.
The Taming of the Shrew (1967), director Franco Zeffirelli.
The Taming of the Shrew (1929), director Sam Taylor.
A Thousand Acres (1997), director Jocelyn Moorhouse.
Throne of Blood (1957), director Akiro Kurosawa.
Twelfth Night (1980), director John Gorrie.
Twelfth Night (1986), director Neil Armfield.
Twelfth Night (1988), directors Kenneth Branagh and Paul Kafno.
Twelfth Night (1996), director Trevor Nunn.

Text

Baldwin, T W (1927), *Organisation and Personnel of the Shakespearean Company*, Princeton, pp229-283.
Bate, J (1997), *The Genius of Shakespeare*, London: Picador.
Boose, Lynda E and Burt, Richard (1997), *Shakespeare, The Movie: Popularising the Plays on Film, TV and Video*, London/New York: Routledge.
Brakhage, Stan (1977), *Film Biographies*, Berkeley, California: Turtle Island.
Brockbank, Philip (1988) *Players of Shakespeare 1*, Cambridge: Cambridge University Press
Bulman, J C and Coursen, H R (eds) (1988), *Shakespeare on Television*, Hanover, N H: University Press of New England.
Chambers, E K (1923), *The Elizabethan Stage*, Oxford: Oxford University Press vol 1, pp270-271.

Collick, John (1989), *Shakespeare, Cinema and Society*, Manchester: Manchester University Press.

Coursen, Herbert E (1997), *Teaching Shakespeare with Film and Television: A Guide*, Westport, Connecticut: Greenwood Press.

Craig, Hardin (ed) (1961), *The Complete Works of Shakespeare*, New York: Scott Foresman.

Davies, Anthony, and Wells, Stanley (eds) (1994), *Shakespeare and the Moving Image: The Plays on Film and Television*, Cambridge: The University Press.

Davis, James E and Salomone, Ronald E (1993), *Teaching Shakespeare Today: Practical Approaches and Productive Strategies*, Urbana, Illinois: National Council of Teachers of English.

Durrant, Calvin (1996), *To Prove a Villain: A Workshop Approach to Richard III*, revised edition, Sydney: St Clair Press.

Friedlander, Larry (1988), "The Shakespeare Project: Experiments in Multimedia Education", *Academic Computing*, 2(7): 20-29; 66-68. (Summary in *The Writing Notebook: Creative Word Processing in the Classroom*, 8(4): 4-6 (1991).)

Griffin, C W (1989), "Teaching Shakespeare on Video", *English Journal* 77(7): 40-43.

Hunter, Evan (1997), *Me and Hitch*, London: Faber.

Kittredge, G L (1940), *The Tragedy of King Lear*, London: Ginn.

Loehlin, James (1997), " 'Top of the World, Ma': *Richard III* and the Cinematic Convention" in Boose, Lynda and Burt, Richard *Shakespeare, the Movie*, London: Routledge.

Mallick, D (1984), *How Tall is This Ghost, John?* Adelaide: Australian Association of Teachers of English.

Manvell, Roger (1979), *Shakespeare and the Film*, South Brunswick, N J: Barnes

McLean, Andrew M (1980), *Shakespeare: Annotated Bibliographies and Media Guide for Teachers*, Urbana, Illinois, National Council of Teachers of English.

McKellen, Ian (1996), *William Shakespeare's Richard III - A Screenplay*, London: Doubleday.

McMurtry, Jo (1994), *Shakespeare Films in the Classroom: A Descriptive Guide*, New York: Archon Books

Olivier, Lawrence (1982), *Confessions of an Actor*, London: Weidenfeld and Nicolson.

Parsons, Keith and Mason, Pamela (eds) (1995) *Shakespeare in Performance*, London: Salamander Books.

Partridge E (1960), *Shakespeare's Bawdy*, New York: Dutton, E P.

Pepper, Frank S (1990), *20th Century Anecdotes*, London: Sphere.

Rothwell, Kenneth S and Melzer, Annabelle Henkin (1990), *Shakespeare on Screen: An International Filmography and Videography*, New York/London: Neal-Schuman.

Spurgeon, Caroline F E (1935/1965), *Shakespeare's Imagery and What It Tells Us*, Cambridge: Cambridge University Press.

Sterne, Richard L (1967), *John Gielgud Directs Richard Burton in Hamlet: A Journal of Rehearsals*, New York: Random House.

Tuska, Jon (1991), *Encounters with film-makers: Eight Career Studies*, New York: Greenwood.

Willis, Susan (1991), *The BBC Shakespeare Plays: Making the Televised Canon*, Chapel Hill, N C: University of North Carolina Press.

Willinsky, J and Bedard, J (1989), *The Fearful Passage: Romeo and Juliet in the High School, A Feminist Perspective*, Ottawa: Canadian Council of Teachers of English.

A Note About the Dates of the Play-Texts

A range of dates has been attributed to most of the plays in this selection. These dates have been identified by scholars from manuscripts and records of the times – not all of which are, themselves, accurately dated. In addition, as Baldwin observes, some of the plays were probably not noted for their initial presentation (not necessarily by the same name) but were later refined. The dates used in this text have been accepted from the scholarship of T W Baldwin (1927) and E K Chambers (1923) as they have been affirmed by the editors of the Oxford edition of the complete works, Stanley Wells and Gary Taylor.